Really Rural

FRENCH 34

Janey Wilks

D&C
David and Charles

A DAVID & CHARLES BOOK
Copyright © David & Charles Limited 2009

David & Charles is an F+W Media, Inc. company
4700 East Galbraith Road
Cincinnati, OH 45236

First published in the UK in 2009

Text copyright © Janey Wilks 2009, unless otherwise credited

A catalogue record for this book is available from the British Library.

ISBN-13: 978-0-7153-3518-5 hardback
ISBN-10: 0-7153-3518-9 hardback

Printed in the UK by C P I Antony Rowe Ltd
for David & Charles
Brunel House   Newton Abbot   Devon

Commissioning Editor: Jane Trollope
Editorial Manager: Emily Pitcher
Editor: Verity Muir
Project Editor: Susan Pitcher
Designer: Mia Farrant
Production Controller: Kelly Smith

Visit our website at www.davidandcharles.co.uk

David & Charles books are a____ _____ _____kshops; alternatively you can
contact our Orde_line on 0870 9908222 or write to us at FREEPO T EX2 110, D&C
Direct, Newton A___t, TQ12 4ZZ (US mail nember UK only). US customers call 800-
289-0963 and ___adian custom_____.

CONTENTS

REALLY RURAL
CUSTOMS

REALLY RURAL
CUSTOMS

There's a lot going on out there, and there always has been. Would a Horn Dance do it for you? A Hocktide? Piano smashing? Actually, piano smashing has disappeared from the rural calendar, but the other two are still going strong. And if it seems surprising to bash up a piano as a competitive team sport rather than putting it on EBay, just think how our forbears would have viewed the MoonWalk for Charity (bras in full view) that is probably happening this year at a village near you. So before you find yourself agreeing with Sydney Smith, fresh from a country visit in Victorian times, 'It is a place with only one post a day. In the country I always fear that creation will expire before tea-time.' Just look at the rural year, and some of the ways in which the rural community has got together, let its hair down and partied.

Easter pace-egging

The scene is Sawrey in the Lake District, and the Jolly-boys are calling on Beatrix Potter or Mrs Heelis as she preferred to be called. Old Betsy Brownbags, Jolly Jack Tar, Lord Nelson, Old Paddy from the Cork and Old Tosspot arrive at Hill Top Farm and sing:

Here's one or two jolly boys all of one mind
We've come a-pace-egging, I hope you'll prove kind
I hope you'll prove kind with your eggs and strong beer
And we'll come no more nigh you until the next year.

From *Folklore and Customs of Rural England*, Margaret Baker

And instead of telling the Jolly-boys exactly where they could put their pace-eggs, Mrs Heelis is reported to have greeted them warmly, with smiles and shillings.

An Easter Pudding

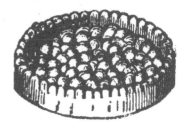

What a nice idea. Let's do it.

'Beat seven eggs, yolks and white separately; add a pint of cream, near the same of spinach-juice, and a little tansy-juice gained by pounding in a stone mortar, a quarter of a pound of Naples biscuit, sugar to taste, a glass of white wine, and some nutmeg. Set all in a sauce-pan, just to thicken, over the fire; then put it into a dish, lined with paste, to turn out, and bake it.'

From *A New System of Domestic Cookery,* Mrs Rundell 1835

If a pint of spinach-juice and a dash of tansy-juice haven't livened the pudding up enough, how about some pink-spiked bistort for that extra kick?

The leaves of the pink-spiked bistort, Easter giant, passion dock or Easter ledger make an extra special Easter pudding, especially famous in the Lake District and often eaten with roast veal.

From *Folklore and Customs,* Margaret Baker

Sounds yummy. But I think I'll have a hot cross bun.

Courting

Spring is traditionally the time for courtship, a time when (to quote William Barnes of Dorset):

The frisken chaps did skip about
An'coose the maidens in and out
From *West Country Words and Ways* K C Phillipps

I bet they did. If the maidens felt that the frisken chaps needed sorting out, here are some helpful words from Billy Treglase, a Cornish rhymester:

All the women of Summercourt Fair,
I'll give'ee advice, then you can beware.
If your man do drink too much beer or gin
You must scat'un down with a rolling pin.

Billy was reported to haunt fairs, singing verse of his own composition. This may have been tiring for some but you feel that he knew his audience.

Mothers against globalization

A true story, from St Keverne, Cornwall:

A visitor found the mother of the house weeping bitterly. In answer to his inquiry, she replied: 'Aw, ais, sir! Why, my daughter is getting married next week!' 'Why are you crying, then,' asked the visitor, 'that's something to rejoice over, surely?' 'Aw dear, no, sir!' she replied with a fresh outburst of grief, 'she's marrying a furriner!' 'Is that so? Is he a Frenchman, a German, or what?' 'My dear life, no!' cried the old lady, ''tes worse than that. Why, maister, he's a Cury man!' (A parish some six miles from St Keverne.)

From *Cornwall and its people*,
A.K. Hamilton Jenkins

Invitation to a Welsh wedding

In rural Wales, when a wedding date was fixed, a gwahoddwr, or bidder, was packed off to invite the guests. He would travel miles around the neighbourhood, proclaiming in every house a long 'bidding poem' or storiwawdd. Here is a prose version of part of an invitation given by a bidder in Llanbadarn in Cardiganshire:

Enion Owain & Llio Elys

With kindness and amity, with decency and liberality for Enion Owain and Llio Elys, he invites you to come with your goodwill on the plate: bring current money; a shilling, two or three, four or five, with cheese and butter. We invite the husband, and wife, and children, and men-servants, from the greatest to the least. Come there early: you shall have victuals freely, and drink cheap, stools to sit on, fish if we can catch them.

Or, in modern parlance: do all come, it's a sit-down meal. The list is with John Lewis and we'd love some mugs, but a Nespresso coffee machine would be even better.

Once the penny post started up, a letter replaced the storiwawdd. Shame.

From *Crafts, Customs and Legends of Wales*, Mary Corbett Harris

LIVELY WEDDINGS

then...

In Llanedy in the early nineteenth century, matters were out of hand. The parson would be bombarded with nuts and apples. 'The easy going clergyman would take no other notice of it than brushing these missiles off the open page of his prayer-book.' But things changed when a new young curate took his first wedding. 'On being struck by some nuts, he looked up, marked a prominent offender, closed his book, jumped over the chancel rails, seized the man, and flung him neck and crop right through the window.' The culprit suffered three broken ribs and not surprisingly the custom ceased forthwith.

At Donnington-on-Bain, Lincolnshire, all the old women of the parish, 'with an ardour unabated by the chill of age', tossed hassocks at the bridal party. And the Rev J Barmby spoke feelingly of a Yorkshire Dales wedding: 'Nothing can be imagined comparable to it in wildness and obstreperous mirth. The bride and bridegroom may possibly be a little subdued, but their friends are like men bereft of reason. They career round the bridal party like Arabs of the desert, galloping over ground on which, in cooler moments, they would hesitate even to walk on a horse – shouting all the time, and firing volleys from the guns they carry with them.

From *Wedding Customs and Folklore*, Margaret Baker

now...

After a memorable stag night in Ibiza, Scott is feeling the worse for wear. Although one eyebrow and half of his hair have been shaved off, he manages to struggle into his wedding finery with the help of his best man, Gazza, and makes it to the church on time. Debs is also feeling second-rate after her hen party in Split (lovely boys, those Croatians), but she's been planning her white wedding for years and rises above the waves of nausea to float to the church in a horse-drawn carriage accompanied by five matching bridesmaids and her mum (in full battle order). The wedding goes nicely, everything very respectful, and at the reception afterwards the alcohol flows freely. Then, just as Scott and Debs are trying to remember how to lead off in the waltz, Deb's uncle takes exception to a remark passed by Gazza in his best man's speech and starts a punch-up on the dance floor, right in the middle of the genuine rose petals. A short, eventful time later, the whole wedding party is ejected from the hotel and Scott and Debs just have time to visit Gazza and Deb's uncle in the police cells before they set off for Stansted Airport.

May Day

The fun continues into May. In 1861 a man found a party of four singers with flute and clarinet on his lawn on May Day in Swinton, North Yorkshire. Although justifiably startled, he rallied quickly and was told the words of two May songs then and there, which he recorded for posterity.

Come listen awhile until what we shall say,
Concerning the season, the month we call May;
For the flowers they are springing, and the birds they do sing,
And the baziers are sweet in the morning of May'.

Noting that 'baziers' or bear's ears are more normally known as auriculas, he doubtless distributed smiles and shillings all round.

Sport

As well as the full range of country sports that involve guns, tweed and group photographs in front of mounds of feather and fur, more gentle outdoor sports have long been embraced in rural circles. Tennis and golf are perennially popular, as are croquet and swimming. In Victorian times the sea-side holiday provided a popular break from rural routine. Here a country vicar has a rush of blood to the head whilst holidaying at the seaside.

'Sea-water had been credited with almost magical properties for many decades – whether bathed in or actually drunk. The seaside holiday, conferring health benefits while providing delightful opportunities for flirtation and other advantages, became an annual event for all who could afford it. Nude bathing for women disappeared early in the reign, though the formal bathing dress was a late invention. Men, on the other hand, habitually bathed nude even in mixed company till towards the end of the century – a curate in 1874 was infuriated to find that at Shanklin, IOW, 'one has to adopt the detestable habit of bathing in drawers. If ladies don't like to see men naked, why don't they keep away from the sight?'

Why indeed?

Some really rural events

If you are upset by waving handkerchiefs, the tinkle of bells and somebody with a bladder on a stick, look away now.

In *Curious Britain* Anthony Burton tells of how he took a Swedish friend down to his local for a pint and there chanced upon the sight of a troop of Morris Men. 'It was difficult to tell whether he was delighted or merely astonished. He had never, he declared, seen anything so bizarre.'

CORNISH BENT

Let us start in Helston, where they are performing the Furry Dance. It's as well to concentrate for this one. Take a deep breath.

The dancers form a column, gentlemen on the left, ladies on the right. The master of ceremonies numbers off the dancers into groups of two couples. While the first part of the tune is being played each gentleman leads his partner forward with his right hand, holding her left hand in a raised position. When the second part is played, the two gentlemen in the group change places, passing by the right, and for four bars turn the other gentleman's lady. For the next four bars the gentlemen change places again and turn their own partners. This movement is repeated all the way down the set.

From *Cornwall and its People*, A.K. Hamilton Jenkins

Committed to memory? Of course, this is the grown-ups' dance, the young people's comes earlier in the day and includes a merry tune with a chorus of:

*With Hal-an-Tow, Rum-ble, O!
for we were up as soon as any
day, O!
And for to fetch the summer home
the summer and the may, O!
For summer is a-come, O! and
winter is a-gone, O!*

The senior dance comes complete with beadles and the Mayor in his golden chain, and is led by a band with a gaily decorated drum. As the dancers pass houses, they ring the door bells and rap the knockers.

It's sounding better by the second. The combination of beadles, gaily decorated drum and licence to ring door bells at random would have many people queuing up to join in the Furry-dance.

Me included.

MORRIS MEN

'The (Morris) dancers, all male, wear white cricket shirts and trousers with bright ribbons or garlands crossing back and chest. Bells are stitched on pieces of coloured leather and bound round the legs. Straw hats, gaily adorned with flowers, are the usual headgear, though cricket caps are worn by some sides and be-flowered toppers are not unknown.'

From *Old English Customs*, Roy Christian

And I haven't included the hobby horse, the fool (bladder-on-stick man), the jester, the man-woman and the boy with a triangle.

Tutti-men and orange scramblers

For something completely different, let us go to the Hocktide, in Hungerford.

Two Tutti-men and an Orange Scrambler set off together. The Tutti-men carry staffs decorated with ribbons and flowers and topped with an orange. The Orange Scrambler wears an evening coat and a tall hat adorned with the tail feathers of a cock pheasant and carries a sack of oranges. The Tutti-men visit the house of every commoner and extract a penny from the men and a kiss from the women, carrying a ladder in case a woman escapes upstairs and needs to be kissed through the window. In exchange for each kiss, an orange from the Orange Scrambler's sack is distributed. He also has the job of sticking new oranges on the staffs as needed. This interesting morning ends with lunch, after which the Tutti-men and Orange Scrambler emerge and throw oranges at a waiting crowd of children.

Of course they do.

The Horn Dance

And while you are still grappling with the unforgettable image of a Tutti-man swarming up a ladder to kiss a coy lady while the **Orange Scrambler** busily squeezes yet another orange onto his staff, come with me to **Abbots Bromley**, where they are performing the **Horn Dance**.

The dance takes place on the Monday after the first Sunday after 4 September Six sets of reindeer antlers are handed out at the church to six dancers wearing Tudor costume, the largest antlers having a spread of 2 feet and going to the chief dancer. The dancers and are accompanied by Fool, hobby horse, bowman, a man dressed in woman's clothing (known as Maid Marian), plus two musicians. Quite why Tudor dress is worn is uncertain. It is possible that the earliest dancers were nude, and that this represents the first costume worn.

From *Curious Britain*, Anthony Burton

Goodness me!
More detail, please.

The dance itself is simple enough. First the six men with horns turn a circle; then the leader turns inwards and passes between the second and third dancers, the others following to form a complete loop. The dancers then face each other in two sets of three. Now comes the climax of the dance. With antlers raised as though to fight, the lines advance, passing left shoulder to left shoulder, the tips of their horns almost touching. After several repetitions the group resumes single file.

From *Curious Britain*, Anthony Burton

Yes, but what about the costumes?

Only the most unbending of traditionalists could object to the introduction of the costumes, which have added a visual attraction to a dance that basically has not altered since it was first described in detail…in 1686. Certainly the villagers themselves are determined to keep faith with tradition. This accounts for the purchase in 1964 of a duplicate set of six horns, insured for £100 each, to be used when the dancing takes place at functions outside Abbots Bromley, for tradition insists that the original horns must not be taken outside the parish.

From *Old English Customs*, Roy Christian

So there we have it. And I think we are all relieved that the unbending traditionalists allow the Horn Dancers to wear costumes, especially in these days of chancy weather.

Crying the Neck

This custom is really, really rural, and comes from a time when the scythe was still **King of the Harvest**, long before the combine harvester trundled into view.

The cutting of the last few handfuls of standing corn in the harvest field was marked by a ceremony known as 'crying the neck'. Gathering towards the centre of the field, the harvesters would divide into three bands, and as the reaper severed the last swath and raised it high above his head, the first group would call forth in stentorian tones: 'We have it! We have it! We have it!' to which the second demanded: 'What 'av 'ee? What 'av 'ee? What 'av 'ee?' the third replying: 'A neck! A neck! A neck!' Then all, together, joined in shouting: 'Hip! Hip! Hip! Hurrah! Hurrah for the neck!'
From *Cornwall and its people*, A.K. Hamilton Jenkins

Then we have another eye-witness report from the fields of North Devon. A gentleman farmer observed the oldest reaper collecting the best ears among the sheaves and plaiting the straw 'very tastefully' into the device of a neck. The men bent low to the stubble, then with a musical cry of 'The neck!' threw their hats in the air and had a brief scuffle for the neck. Whoever managed to snatch it, shot into the farmhouse and tried to kiss the dairymaid. If she spotted him first, and presumably if he wasn't her type, she could throw a large pail of water all over him.

A pretty scene and good clean fun. But it crossed my mind that a stranger wandering innocently onto the farm on the last day of harvest a few centuries earlier, when more blood-thirsty customs prevailed, might have discovered that he had made a serious mistake. A fatal mistake, even.

What 'ave 'ee?'
A neck! A neck! A neck!'
Plaited straw or a stranger's?'
Imm.

THE RURAL ORGANISER

Pam is a born organizer. The village, tuned to take full advantage of incoming voluntary labour, recognized this the moment she arrived at the Old Dairy, sorted out her new house within days and threw a 'Hello to my New Neighbours!' party. Turn-out at the party was disappointing but the drive behind the initiative was noticed in the village's corridors of power. Over Sunday lunchtime drinks at the Royal Oak, the Brigadier remarked to David (resting Hedge Fund Manger) and Simon (incredibly rich GP) that the new arrival at the Old Dairy seemed to know how to get things going. And they agreed. Doors were opened, and after a polite interval Pam moved rapidly up the ranks of the Parish Council, the Parochial Church Council and the management board of the Fluffy Bunnies Under-Fives Playgroup. The cherry on the cupcake of her plans for her new village was to join and eventually chair the Village Fete Committee, which she achieved within two years. Joyce, the outgoing chairman, had presided over a pleasant and very local little event whose

White Elephant Stall and Second Hand Book
Stall usually managed to send £100 profit to the
local children's hospice. Joyce jumped just before
she was pushed, and watched with astonishment as
Pam's new version of the Village Fete, now called the
Country Fayre, was announced on local radio, opened by
a local celebrity and culminated in a mass launch of hot
air balloons. After damages had been paid to Greg, the farmer, for mental
distress caused to his dairy herd who stampeded in a body when the first
balloon was inflated, there was still enough profit to refurbish an entire wing
of the local children's hospice. Pam is tireless, and the village are beginning
to realize that they have a tiger by the tail. Now she plans to stage a 'Son
et Lumière' at the parish church with massed folk dancing. The Vicar hides
when Pam approaches.

A good night out

then...

There's a turkey-plucking evening in the village hall. There will be lemonade and a tea urn. Lots of friends and neighbours are going. You dig out your thick apron and a headscarf and head off, expecting a jolly time out with gossip and singing.

now...

There's a 'Singalong to the Sound of Music' film night in the village hall. An alcoholic licence has been obtained at enormous expense. Lots of friends and neighbours are going. You dig out your lederhosen, or white dress with blue satin sash, and head off, expecting a jolly night out with gossip and singing.

Michaelmas

Now the harvest is home, the nights are drawing in and the rural year is heading towards its culmination with the joys of Christmas. But while Autumn is still with us, let us witness a Michaelmas Hiring Fair, and listen to the farmers asking a particularly unusual question.

Mrs Baker writes of her mother's girlhood in Canterbury, Kent, about 1868.

'She told me how she always enjoyed going to the Michaelmas Hiring Fair, where she liked to listen to the farmers re-engaging their labourers for another spell of work. They would walk up to particular workers who had satisfied them during past service and say, 'Pawk agin, er'ow?'. Her father explained that this was 'Pork again or how?' i.e. 'Will you have pork again with me, or what will you do?'

From *Folklore and Customs of Rural England*

I can think of many answers to this particular question, but none of them would be likely to result in gainful employment.

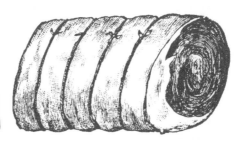

Christmas

Next time you are clashing trolleys in the supermarket with a week to go before Christmas, when the queue for the tills stretches to the frozen food department and they are out of satsumas again, consider Christmas preparations in Yorkshire circa 1898.

'There is the pudding to make and partly boil; all the ingredients for the plum-cake to order; the mincemeat to prepare for the mince-pies; the goose to choose from some neighbouring farmer's stock; the cheese to buy; and the wheat to have the hullins beaten off and to cree, for the all-important frumenty; the yule-cake or pepper-cake to make; the hollin to gather.'

From *Folklore and Customs of Rural England*

Brussels sprout peeling for twelve and a celebrity chef's chestnut, lemongrass and blueberry stuffing to make? Or escorting your wheat to have the hullins beaten? Either way, it's a busy old time.

Recipe for mince pies on a grand scale

From 'Anne Andrews her Book', a recipe book started in 1756. The quantities make modern recipes seem positively minimalist.

3lb suet cut very fine

2lb currants, nicely pick'd, wash'd, rubb'd and dried by the fire

½lb fine sugar pounded fine

½ pint of brandy

½ pint of sack

2lb raisins stoned and chopped very small

Half a hundred of fine pippins, pared, cored and chopp'd small

¼ oz mace

¼ oz cloves

2 large nutmegs all beat fine

Mix all well together and pit it down close in a stone pot, and it will keep good 4 months. When made into pies put citron and orange peel.

then...

On Christmas Day at Dynefawr Castle, Carmarthenshire, everyone assembled in the great hall. The poorest women of varying ages, carefully selected from the village, came in and were allowed to choose either a large round of beef, a huge roll of Welsh flannel, or some blankets. In return, each woman presented a rosy apple, garlanded with holly berries, on three wooden skewers. The apples were never eaten but were stored in the housekeeper's room till Twelfth Night, then thrown away.

From *Crafts, Customs and Legends of Wales,* Mary Corbett Harris

Mince pies must be tasted by all – 'every mince pie eaten away from home means a happy month to come' but pies, made in twelves to strengthen the charm, must be offered by a friend.

From *Folklore and Customs of Rural England*

In the farms and inns of Devon and Somerset the yule-log's place was taken by the ashen faggot, bound with nine withes and lighted with charred twigs from last year's Christmas hearth. The bursting of each band called for a quart of cider and toasts were drunk while the company jumped in sacks and ducked for apples and the great yule candle (which must be a gift and was often presented by the family's chandler) lighted at the dinner table by the master of the house, burned steadily through the night.

From *Folklore and Customs of Rural England*

CIDRE MOUSSEUX

All over the country bands of friends and relations gather together and present each other with scented candles and striped socks. The table groans with an outsize turkey stuffed with many exotic fruits, then crackers are pulled and festive paper hats are worn while diverse strange jokes are exchanged and wondered over. After the boiled pudding (set alight amidst much rejoicing) all sit on sofas and watch the Queen's speech and sundry time-honoured televised films.

The trappings that surround it may evolve over the years, but the Spirit of Christmas doesn't change much.

Come let me taste your Christmas beer
That is so very strong,
And I do wish that Christmas time
With all its mirth and song
Was twenty times as long.

From *Cornwall and its people*, A.K. Hamilton Jenkins

REALLY RURAL
CHARACTERS

REALLY RURAL
CHARACTERS

Rural living seems to bring out character. People who stand tall and state their opinions fearlessly, or invent something amazing, or prepare to fight to the death over gooseberry weights. Anthony Burton says: 'Everyone must, I imagine, at some time or other have had the experience of walking…along a country lane and suddenly being confronted by something that stops you in your tracks. 'Good lord,' you exclaim, 'what an extraordinary object.' Replace the object with the person and there you have the characters that fill the following pages. They are extraordinary. It must be the country air.

Three outstanding characters

There is nobody better to start with than Mr Theophilus Smith, as described by Philip A Wright in *Old Farm Implements*. Mr Smith of Hill Farm, Attleborough, Norfolk, had been working on modifications to plough design, and his ideas were noticed by the Earl of Albemarle, Master of Horse and a local landowner. The Earl arranged that Mr Smith should take his models to Windsor Castle and show them to Queen Victoria. And this is where it gets good.

The hour was late when Theophilus arrived at Windsor Castle. A Gentleman of the Household with the rank of Colonel received him and suggested that Theophilus spent the night at an inn. The honest farmer was indignant and replied: *'that do seem mighty queer, that's both ill-convenient and costly. I was commanded to come here and the least you can do is to give me a bed. If you was to come to Attleborough my missus would find you a bed, 'specially if we'd asked you to come; and if you was as hungry as I be, I warrant he'd find you something to eat.'*

I am glad to report that the Colonel found him lodging at the Castle and presumably something to fill the Inner Man as well. The next day Mr Smith was ushered into the Royal Presence, who could not have been nicer.

First came Prince Albert who allowed the plough to be called after him, then the Queen herself. They had a nice chat about ploughs, wages, cottages and the poor. Then the conversation continued. He had expected a person 'with a gold sceptre in her hand and her gown all a-trailing behind, as we see in the picters; but she was a comely, simple woman with a kind look'.

Queen Victoria *How did you come to think of this clever invention?*
Theophilus   *Well your Majesty, I had it in my head for a sight of days before it would come straight. I saw what was wanted well enough, but I couldn't make out how to get it. At last I made it a matter of prayer, and one morning it came like a flash.*
Queen Victoria *Why, do you pray about your plough?*
Theophilus   *Well there, Mum, why shouldn't I? I mind one of my boys when he was a little mite, I bowt him a whip and rarely pleased he was. Well, he comes to me one day crying as if his heart would break. He'd broken the whip.*

Well now Your Majesty, Mum, that whip was nothing to me but it was something to see tears running down my boy's cheeks, so I took him on my knee and comforted him. 'Now don't you cry', said I. 'I'll mend your whip I will so that it will crack as ever.' Well now, don't you think our Father in Heaven cares as much for me as I care for my boy? My plough wasn't of much consequence to Him, but I know my trouble was.

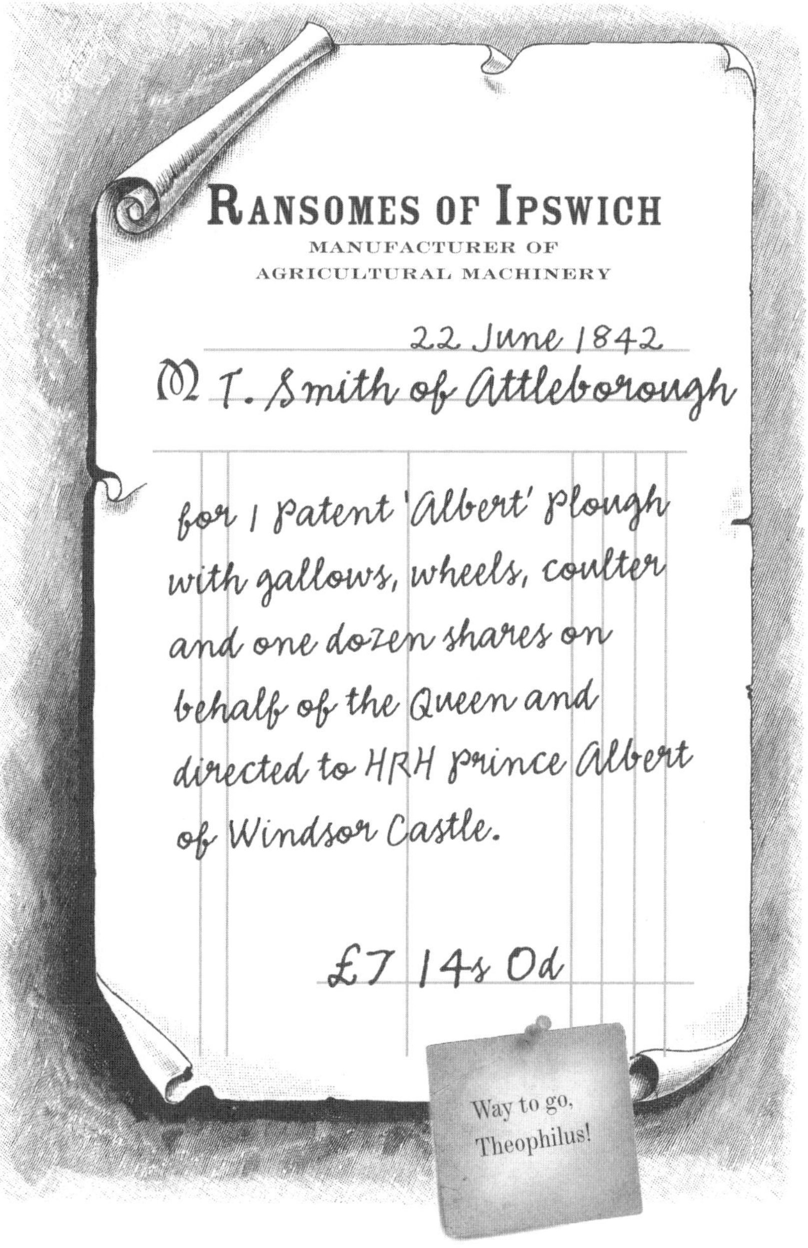

Ransomes of Ipswich

MANUFACTURER OF
AGRICULTURAL MACHINERY

22 June 1842

M T. Smith of Attleborough

for 1 patent 'Albert' plough with gallows, wheels, coulter and one dozen shares on behalf of the Queen and directed to HRH Prince Albert of Windsor Castle.

£7 14s 0d

Way to go, Theophilus!

Mr J.H.B. Peel

Now for another man who will not be silenced. In several books, J.H.B. Peel leads us authoratively around the roads of Britain. He knows his subject and writes eruditely and informatively about the passing landscapes. To start with, he regrets the traffic (he is in a car himself) but makes the best of a bad job. But then you find him getting twitchy.

It was during a traffic-jam that I suddenly remembered William the Conqueror and the Domesday Book. The village green is still there; so also are the venerable homes and a church with a shingle spire; but cars encompass them, and repose has fled.

As his journey continues things really begin to get to him, although it is still just a grumble beneath the breath.

Posterity may marvel that each year we either killed or wounded hundreds of thousands of Britons in road 'accidents'; and that while our enemies grew stronger, we chose to grow weaker, squandering borrowed money on alcohol, narcotics, and gambling.

Never mind posterity – Mr Peel is building up a good head of steam, not helped when he reaches the Lake District, winds down his car window, and discovers that other people have got there first. He savagely paraphrases his beloved Wordsworth, who had admiringly summed up the Lake District as:

'a sort of national property, in which every man has a right and interest who has an eye to perceive and a heart to enjoy'.

Wiping the froth from his lips, Mr Peel does his best to contain his ire by describing the unhappy scene as follows:

'The Lake District is a sort of national property, in which every man has a right and interest to drive a car, acquire a weekend cottage, perpetrate motorways, petrol pumps, caravan sites, lucky charm shops, fish-and-chipperies, Bingo bars and car parks'.

Fore-and-aft the motionless cars sweated in sunlight, their tin-ware stabbing the eye. Fingers tapped impatient steering wheels. Children grizzled. Women yawned. Dogs panted. Suddenly the crocodile jerked forward a few yards, then wavered, creaked, and once more halted.

We've all been there. But it is not traffic that makes Mr Peel finally draw himself up to full height, turn to face his audience and really let rip. It is the Common Market and its associated uniformity.

Though I admire Goethe, and delight in Ronsard, I will not follow their businesslike descendants into the Graeco-Roman jargon of a common market-place. For a thousand years the men of this kingdom have measured Time and Space in miles and inches, in midday and midnight. I was born an Englishman, and I shall die an Englishman, speaking my native language, not lisping the cosmopolitan Shibboleths of Mammon.

Just try lisping 'the cosmopolitan Shibboleths of Mammon' and you'll see that Mr Peel has a point. It is not easy.

Fortunately for all concerned, J.H.B. Peel finally finds his personal heaven during a rainstorm, on foot this time, and among people he could do business with.

At about six o'clock the sky darkened, the breeze dropped, the storm broke, and I ran for shelter. 'Well,' said the farmer's wife, 'we don't really take visitors unless we know them. But you'd better come inside.' The rafters of the living room were blacker than ebony; the hearth was fragrant with cherry wood. Two boiled eggs arrived, both brown; honey from the bees, bread from the oven, ham from the piggery. There followed three hours of fireside talk with people who, if they governed England, would soon bring most of us to our senses, and the rest to an emigration office. At ten o'clock the staircase creaked, the bath boiled, the mattress feathered, the rain ceased, the owl hooted, the silence sang, and the truant slept.

At last! But it must have been an incandescent three hour talk over the boiled eggs and honey.

Mad Jack Fuller

Time to move on to a man who lived life exactly as he wanted to. Meet Mad Jack Fuller, of Brightling Park, in Sussex. Mr Fuller weighed over twenty stone, it has been admiringly reported, and was a serial folly-builder in the nineteenth century.

SUGAR LOAF

So named because of its resemblance to a sugar loaf (naturally).

Mad Jack's friends challenged his statement that he could see the spire of Dallington Church from his home in Brightling Park, and he was proved wrong. He duly paid up; then, to satisfy a whim, caused an exact replica of the spire to be built by the roadside at Woods Corner, so situated that from his window it appeared to be rising from the ridge. 'At least I can see it now,' he said; 'and no one can tell one from t'other.' In general terms he was right in this.

From *Curious Britain*, Anthony Burton

An alternative version of the story has him leaping from the dining table when he was out with friends and rushing home to check whether his boast that he could see the church spire from his dining-room window was a good one. Discovering that the view was blocked by a hill, he had the fake spire built at top speed and won his bet. Either way, the spire is there, and either way it's a great story.

FIT FOR PURPOSE

Tradition has it that Mad Jack Fuller used this curious and comfortless place to entertain lady-friends of a class and type that he could not well admit to his residence. But, in view of his size, it is questionable whether he could pass through the constricted entrance, whether alone or accompanied by the lady of his current choice.

Ibid,

I say! On to Mad Jack's next folly.

THE BRIGHTLING NEEDLE

Apparently built because Cleopatra's Needle had just been presented to Britain to mark the coronation of George IV and Jack wanted to show the world that anything the Egyptians could do, could be done just as well by a Sussex squire.

From *Curious Britain,* Anthony Burton

OBSERVATORY

A small temple built in the form of a rotunda and observatory, this, it was said, was not built for observation of the stars but for observation of Fuller himself. His servants were expected to stay there during their master's absence at Westminster where he was MP, to keep an eye open for the first appearance of the carriage bringing him home. Then they were to dash from the observatory to the house to get everything ready for his arrival: slippers warmed, hot meal ready, glass filled.

GREAT WALL
Built to relieve unemployment.

HERMITAGE
Built for a hermit. But he couldn't persuade one to occupy it.

HIS FINEST AND LAST

Fuller owned most of the village, including the pub. This was called the Fuller's Arms and became a handy stopping-off point for parishioners on their way to church. The vicar asked if the pub could be moved, and Fuller agreed on the condition that he could design his own tomb. So a new pub was built at a safe distance from the church, and Fuller had a wonderful time constructing an enormous stone pyramid in the churchyard. He was finally interred in his pyramid in 1834 at the age of seventy-seven, apparently sitting in his favourite chair in front of a laden table.

I think we like Jack Fuller.

A FINE SET OF DIRECTIONS

A doctor, holidaying in the north of Scotland, was given the name of a ghillie who might give him a day's fishing. He stopped at a village to ask for directions, and here they are.

The very elderly shopkeeper asked who he wanted to visit and told him: 'You take the road out of the village and turn left at the crossroads. About six miles on you'll come to a croft. He doesn't live there. A mile further on there is another croft and he doesn't live there either. But another mile on there's a third croft. And that's where you'll find his widow.'

From *Memoirs of a Ghillie*, Gregor MacKenzie

...and a silly story about Old Charlie Boyer, who got owled:

Old Charlie Boyer went out and got tight, and couldn't find his way home. Going through Staple Park an owl hooted, 'Hooo, hooo?' Charlie replied, 'Charlie Boyer, hay-maker, tatie-digger, wants to go to Whitford Sir, honest a man as ever broke bread.' But all the owl replied was, Hooo, hooo.'

Very silly. And yet there is something majestic about Charlie's recital of his abilities and attributes under pressure, even when drunk as an owl.

Some more characters

Continuing the folly theme, this story features an unnamed admiral raking the horizon with his telescope, searching for reasons to be offended. The folly in question is Lord Berner's Folly at Faringdon, built in 1935. Here comes the admiral, shouldering through the crowd of objectors.

A retired admiral appeared for the opposition, claiming that the tower would obstruct the view from his house. When the lawyers for Lord Berner attempted to parry his arguments by pointing out that the admiral could only see the tower at all if he looked through a telescope, the admiral expressed himself astonished by the defence argument. Of course, he declared, it was only visible through a telescope, but how else would they expect an admiral to view scenery?

From *Shell Book of Curious Britain*

The tower was built anyway. Men have walked the plank for less.

MR BOON OF CLEETHORPES.

In 1956 the Town Council of Cleethorpes, Lincs, who were disappointed with the over-cautious Whitsun forecast of that year, appointed one of their own nightwatchmen, Mr Harry Boon, to issue daily forecasts based on his lifelong observations of the flights of birds and insects, and it was agreed that from the beginning of August until the end of the summer Mr Boon's predictions should be compared with the official forecasts to see who was the more accurate. Harry Boon won the competition. He was presented with a memento by the Mayor and given a free holiday, which he chose to spend in Cleethorpes.

From *Britain's Weather,* David Bowen

What a great man. What loyalty to Cleethorpes. Majorca, eat your heart out!

I feel that our next character would have got on like a house in fire with J.H.B. Peel (see page 41). He is just described as an 88-year-old Dartmoor cottager but, as he pins you to the wall with a gnarled forefinger, you instinctively feel that here is somebody else who wouldn't have much truck with the cosmopolitan Shibboleths of Mammon:

Well, Mister Someone, these people come down here and take us all to be fools. They come down here to forget what they've created elsewhere, and do exactly the same. They can keep their money and their fancy ways. I believe I'm living on the right side of the hedge, and no-one can tell me different.

From *The Right Side of the Hedge,* Chris Chapman

ON THE SUBJECT OF GOOSEBERRIES

Meanwhile, Mr W Gordon Cragg is approaching boiling point on the subject of gooseberries.

I read an article recently by Trevor Holloway entitled 'Gooseberry Show and Tub Race' on which I feel that I must comment. He writes a lot of nonsense. He says, 'As far as is known, only one such show has survived – at Egton, near Whitby, Yorkshire.' He also goes on to mention that the heaviest single gooseberry was nearly 4oz. This I can assure him is quite impossible. As the Honorary Secretary of the Mid Cheshire Gooseberry Shows Association I should like to inform Mr Holloway that his statement is quite wrong. In our Association we have seven shows. Members of these shows total at least 120 and live in the area bounded by Lower Peover, Over Peover, Marton, Lower Withington, Swettenham, Goostrey and Holmes Chapel. For many years our members have been aggrieved by the information on gooseberry growing emanating from the Egton area, especially about the weights of gooseberries grown. Referring to the heaviest single gooseberry – in 1852 one named 'London' weighed 37 pennyweights and 7 grains, which is a few grains over 2 ounces, and since then the heaviest one has been a Woodpecker grown by Mr T Blackshaw in 1937. I do hope you will be kind enough to pass on my comments to Mr Holloway, and if he wishes to learn something about gooseberry growing I am sure some of our members will gladly oblige.

From *A Guide to Country Living*, ed P.D.N. Earle

Wow, what a broadside! There is material there for years of highly enjoyable acrimonious exchange of correspondence between the Gooseberry Show Associations. As Mr Somebody also learned, you meddle with rural life at your peril, and there will always be a Mr W Gordon Cragg to pick you up on a mistake.

Really Rural Today

THE RURAL PROTESTER

Derek is a thorn in the side of local bureaucracy. Every time an unpopular housing quota has to be filled, or a contentious application is to be considered, the planning department heaves a deep sigh and braces itself for Derek. He knows just how to access documents on their website, and has an encyclopaedic knowledge of the latest planning laws. A housing estate planned for a field that the River Splatt has flooded on a regular basis for time out of mind? The tentative prod of light industry, where Derek feels no light industry should be? Derek is on the case, and he acts with the speed of a striking python. Derek knows when to petition, and when the moment has arrived to grasp a placard firmly and march up and down in front of regional television cameras. He gives a good radio interview: fact-filled and direct. He knows how to mobilise a vocal local pressure group. He may ruffle feathers, on both sides, but it is partly thanks to Derek that his particular patch of countryside remains an Area of Outstanding Natural Beauty.

Mr William Barnes

While one strong rural character is loudly seeing off all comers, another (just as strong) will be quietly doing good. Meet William Barnes: poet, philologist, schoolmaster, historian, walker and parish priest.

He was born near Sturminster Newton in Dorset. He became a village schoolmaster; married happily for life; contrived (by overworking and under-eating) to start a school of his own at Mere in Wiltshire; sent himself up to Cambridge at the age of thirty-seven; took Holy Orders; was appointed Rector of Winterborne Came in Dorset; and, when it was too late to do much good, received a Civil List pension in recognition of his achievement as a poet. His daughter left an endearing picture of the white-bearded parson-poet: 'Sometimes he took a fancy to mow his own lawn but the use of the little mowing machine never gave him the same feeling as did the scythe of his earlier years making its graceful curves.'

From *An Englishman's Home*, J.H.B. Peel

His poetry tends to be written in impenetrable Dorset dialect, this is from *The Child and the Mowers*:

For he died
while the hay
russled grey
On the staddle so
leately begun:
Lik' the mown-grass
a-dried by the day
— Aye! The zwath-
flow'r's a-kill'd by
the sun.

Isn't that lovely? I'm not quite sure, but I think something sad has happened.

Mr Richard Jefferies

Another naturalist and historian was Richard Jefferies who lived near Swindon in Wiltshire. Mr Jefferies could lay a hedge, plough a meadow, make a bid, assess a crop, was a labourer in his father's fields and a reporter on country newspapers. He was regarded as one of the foremost historians of late-Victorian farm life, but sometimes his writing would lapse into mysticism.

The great sun burning with light; the strong, dear earth; the warm sky; the pure air: all filled me with a rapture, an ecstasy, an inflatus.'
from *An Englishman's Home*, J.H.B. Peel

I say, steady on old chap.

More character snapshots

We don't hear much about these men, but what we do hear tends to stick in the mind

JOHN READ

The circular form (of the oast house) was established by John Read, an ingenious gardener who turned his attention to hop-drying after experimenting with methods of heating hothouses and inventing the stomach pump.
From *A History of Farm Buildings in England and Wales*, Nigel Harvey

Inventor of the circular oasthouse and the stomach pump: what an unforgettable combination.

HAGAN SMART

Hagan Smart was a shepherd who lived in a cottage called 'Norway House'. His father had been a very good ice skater and went over to Norway to skate. He earned enough money there to build the house. Hagan was always thinking about ducks; he was always talking about ducks; he claimed that he always dreamed about ducks!
From *Memoirs of a Fen Tiger*, Audrey James

CAL

He was a little man and he travelled from farm to farm with an enormous Suffolk Punch. You had only to look over the stable door for the animal to lay back its ears and bare his teeth. I always felt that had I dared to go in he would have eaten me. One day I asked Cal how it was that he could easily handle this great monster. He explained that if you really want to befriend any animal you should take a slice of bread and sweat it under your arm for a while before feeding it to the animal.

From *Gamekeeper*, John Foyster & Keith Proud

A little man, a huge horse, and some sweaty bread to tame it. You heard it here first.

Evening up the score, just a little

The keen-eyed observer will have noted that every character mentioned in this chapter so far has been male. Rural life was a touch unreconstructed until relatively recently. See how women were occupied while men, in this case shepherds, got on with being characters.

Throughout the day, the wives, sisters, mothers and daughters of the men concerned play a vital part in sustaining spirits and energies. Meat pies, fresh bread and scones, tea and coffee are spread out while activity ceases for a few minutes, and new supplies of cold drinks are left for the sweating men.

From *The Hill Shepherd*, Edward Hart

Not much time, then, for a woman to do more than bake another mound of meat pies on which the returning heroes could feast.

Beatrix Potter, however, bucked the system when she earned enough money from her writing to buy her own property at Hill Top Farm at Sawrey in Westmoreland, and run her own life. She married a local solicitor, Mr William Heelis, against her parents' advice, when she was fifty years old and went her own way from then on. She became a local character and legend. J.H.B. Peel tells us:

I used to spend a part of each year in Westmorland at no great distance from Hill Top, and I met several people who had known Beatrix Potter. 'She were a gurt walker,' one said, 'thought nowt on't weather. And nowt on't clothes neither. I've seen th'owd girl wi' a bit o' sack for a shawl agin't blizzard.' 'Aye,' said another, 'and I'll tell thee summat else. If thee were a tramp, and knocked on't door o' Hill Top, the servant had orders to gie thee a sup o' tea and a silver coin. And didn't the tramps know it!'

And it must have pleased Mrs Heelis, who preferred to be known by her married name, that she was revered locally for her expertise with Herdwick sheep rather than her books about rabbits. Even though the rabbits gave her the freedom to farm her sheep.

Books? Aye she wrote books all right. But we thought more on't when she took to 'Erdwicks. She were a gurt one wi' sheep, were owd Mrs 'Eelis.'

from *An Englishman's Home*, JHB Peel.

REALLY RURAL
ANIMALS

REALLY RURAL
ANIMALS

The country scene comes completely jam-packed with animals, a word I use in the broadest sense. Whether we are discussing an ox called Lusty, a jackdaw up a chimney, a garden full of moles or a witheret (see end of chapter), they are the warp and woof of rural life. Particularly the woof. Speaking of which, here is an opportunist dog.

Driving back after lunch I saw in the middle of a main road, on the brow of the hill, what looked like a dog-fight. A closer approach showed a long-haired dog wriggling violently on its back on a 3ft sewer grating. A nearby textile dye-house had evidently just emptied a vat into the drain, and the dog was enjoying a Turkish bath in the rising clouds of steam.
From *The Countryman Animal Book*, B and M Campbell

Feline tips

Staying with domestic pets for the moment, here is some thrifty advice on how not to spoil your cat.

If you own a kitten, don't spoil it. Be sure to bring it up to have wide and sophisticated tastes in its personal eating habits. A choosey cat can cost you a small fortune in cat foods. But, in the right hands, and if started young enough, a cat may acquire a taste for beans, bacon rind, sprouts, stale cheese, scraps of old bread and butter and cold tea, as well as meat pieces of every kind.
From *1001 Ways of Saving Money*, Tony Swindells

Alternatively the cat may decide to distance itself permanently from the provider of sprouts and cold tea, and instead to patronize a household with regular supplies of Dainty Cat Chicken Pate. From a tin.

More dodgy advice on the subject of cats, this time Victorian.

You did quite right to try the sulphur ointment, and you may still use it for about a fortnight; if the cat's hair does not show signs of returning naturally then use a dressing of mild ammonia liniment once a day. It may be improved by the addition of a little tincture of Spanish flies.
From *Oh No Dear!*, comp. Roy Hindle

Tincture of Spanish flies? I am reasonably confident that, over a hundred years ago, a hairless Victorian cat was seen streaking away to a more congenial establishment.

Blackberry picking, in company

Horses have long been revered in the country, as companions, beasts of burden and for their sheer beauty. But they can have whimsical moods, and it is one thing to admire a convention of horses from the safe side of a hedge and quite another to find yourself up close and personal, when the only thing between you and all those hooves is a frail basket of blackberries...

You will discover that everything is wringing wet, as drenching cascades are unleashed over you each time you touch so much as a leaf; and that some domestic animals are particularly inquisitive and aggressive before breakfast, and they will constitute the main hazards. Horses, looming up at you through the swirling morning mists, affect fey attitudes, and have a quirky sense of humour. It can be disconcerting if you have safely negotiated a wet and treacherous nettle-stuffed ditch, and are poised on the opposite bank among a mass of superlative blackberries, to find yourself gazing through a frail barrier of willow-wands into the larky faces of a couple of horses with the wind in their ears. If you say to them 'Go away', and they go not, and you know that quite soon you are going to overbalance, and fall through the frail willows and land among their massed legs and hooves, you must resist the urge to shout at them rudely and angrily, but withdraw and proceed backwards through the treacherous ditch.

From *The Countryman Book of Humour*, ed. Margaret Campbell

Quite right too. There is something very regal about a horse and I should think that crawling backwards from the Presence would go down well.

The oxen chain

Perhaps we had better move on to oxen who are not famed for their fey attitude. For a great many centuries oxen were the animal equivalent of tractors in rural life. Here they are being yoked up:

During the midday meal, which the men generally ate in the fields, the oxen were released from their yokes and turned on to the grass. As soon as they were wanted again the ploughboy had only to shout: 'Young, yoke!' and the ox referred to would at once look up from his grazing and come of his own accord to the plough where he would stand patiently waiting for the yoke to be fixed. In order to keep the oxen in good humour it was customary for the boys to keep singing their names in a drawling fashion almost the whole day long. In the busy seasons of the year their voices could have been heard thus throughout the whole countryside, from dawn to dusk.'

From *Cornwall and its People*, A.K. Hamilton Jenkins

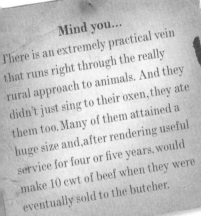

Mind you...
There is an extremely practical vein that runs right through the really rural approach to animals. And they didn't just sing to their oxen, they ate them too. Many of them attained a huge size and, after rendering useful service for four or five years, would make 10 cwt of beef when they were eventually sold to the butcher.

Ode to a tractor

So the tractor's growl may have taken over from the ploughboy's song to his oxen in the countryside, but there must be less of a sentimental tug on the heartstrings when a worn out tractor is dragged off to the breaker's yard. Or perhaps the practically minded ploughboy would happily celebrate the recycling of his ox with a nice beef dinner, whereas now he just trails off to the pub for a ploughman's.

YOU COULDN'T MAKE IT UP

Oxen were always yoked together in the same pairs, and their names tended to come in pairs too: Young and Lusty, Sport and Pleasure, Butler and Steward, Brisk and Lively. But get a load of the old farmer in the Meneage district of Cornwall, who more than a hundred years ago called his team of eight oxen: Rule and Reason, Time and Season, Sweat and Labour, Madcap and Shaver.

Although, as we have already seen, T-bone and Half Pounder might have been more to the point.

THOUGHT FOR THE DAY

There is nothing more exasperating than being ignored by your own cow when you try to call her up from the farthest corner of the pasture at milking time, when it is raining and you have to plod out there and round her up.

From *Keeping a Cow*, Val Spreckley

Intelligent sheep

And now to sheep. Not just any sheep. Here we come on to the vexed question of Jacob's Sheep.

This is a breed whose popularity is increasing rapidly, especially among those who wish to keep just a few animals... They are alert, intelligent and friendly, which is saying a lot for sheep.

From *The Complete Guide to Country Living*,
Suzanne Beedell & Barbara Hargreaves

This is certainly high praise. But just look at what happens when a slur is cast upon the breed.

Q Where can I buy Jacob's Sheep? Can you give me any information about them?

A They are not nearly as good as Scotch half-breeds but might be more prolific. They have a mottled coat which does not sell well.

Whoops! In some far corner of the land a reader is smoking at the ears and reaching for his pen.

Pros and cons of intelligent sheep

A list of the advantages of Jacob's Sheep follows some sharp words from an expert.

A considerable amount of tommy-rot has been recently talked about Jacob's Sheep. As I have had 43 years experience of keeping these sheep, may I be permitted to put this breed before your readers in its proper perspective?

From *A Guide to Country Living*, ed. P.D.N. Earle

Will do on any soil. I recently took my ewes from a heavy clay Dorset farm to a Welsh border farm of lightest soil. They throve and fed excellent. Very quiet indeed, and need no dog to control them. The breed can be absolutely recommended to persons without shepherds. NB Buy two or three horned ewes if possible.

Ibid.

Buy two or three, buy lots of them, even if you haven't got shepherds. But never, ever cast aspersions on Jacob's Sheep.

Strong words against sheep

There must be something about sheep that brings out the vocabulary – now we hear from an anxious person asking for advice after an unfortunate exchange with a local expert.

Q Farmer A owns some ewes and rams, and these are kept by Farmer B. B provides all the keep and hand feed, medicines, dip, etc, and pays vet fees. For shearing, dippings and dagging, each farmer provides one or two men. What do you think would be a fair distribution of the proceeds of wool and lamb sales at the end of twelve months?

Right. Calculator ready?

A In our opinion, a fair distribution would be 2/7 to 5/7; ie 2/7 to A, 5/7 to B or 1/3 to A, 2/3 to B.

Eh?

Q I have about 6 acres of reasonably good grazing, about to be cut for hay. A neighbouring farmer has suggested that I might do worse than keep a few sheep: he rather poo-poohed my protests.

He didn't! Strong words about sheep, a subject that arouses strong passions.

Shepherd's counting

Now ditch the calculator, and adopt the shepherd's method.

1 yan	11 yan-a-dick
2 tyan	12 tyan-a-dick
3 tethera	13 tether-a-dick
4 methera	14 mether-a-dick
5 pimp	15 bumfit
6 sethera	16 yan-a-bumfit
7 lethera	17 tyan-a-bumfit
8 hovera	18 tether-a-bumfit
9 dovera	19 mether-a-bumfit
10 dick	20 giggot

When the shepherd has reached twenty, he puts up one finger and starts again. When he has five fingers up he has reached a hundred and puts a pebble in his pocket.

From *The Hill Shepherd*, Edward Hart

Pimp – dick – bumfit – giggot. I cannot see how any part of this could be improved.
The words, the finger and the pebble seem perfect in every detail to me.

THE HOBBY FLOCK

Twinkle, Tansy, Cocoa and Crumble
are disgracefully spoilt, and that is how
they like it. Chosen from a large flock of
Shetland Sheep at an early age for their
pastel shades and friendly dispositions,
they have consolidated on their position
ever since. They are picky eaters – hay
must be top-grade racehorse hay or else they will just pull it
out of the manger and tread on it. They will only eat hard feed if it is organic,
unbelievably expensive and comes out of pretty bags decorated with naïve
sheep prints. If their fences develop the smallest loop-hole, they escape
immediately and head like homing bees for the local gardening expert's
garden, where they feverishly stuff themselves with rare perennials until
collected by their embarrassed owner. Then they have to be checked over by
the vet in case they ate something poisonous (they are not stupid, and didn't).

For Twinkle and company, the shepherding calendar comes gold-plated.
Instead of being shoved about on the industrial conveyor belt of shearing by
a sweating band of Aussies, they are gently relieved of their fleeces by Baz, a
champion hand-shearer (mechanized shears are noisy, and upset them). As
Baz stuffs a wad of ten pound notes into his back pocket, he reflects happily
that thanks to hobby flocks like this, he can go off for his annual back-
packing trip to Peru a couple of months early. And instead of lambing in the
bleak mid-winter, so that lambs are ready for market at the optimum time,
our hobby flock gives birth in May, when it's warm and there are flowers and
butterflies. The 'c' word ('commercial') is banned. With a stocking rate of one
sheep per acre of impeccably maintained grassland and the finest medical
care, they will live to an enormous age, adored by their owner to the end.

Guess the animal

Can you guess what these are?

- Pigmy pouters
- Dragoons
- Nuns
- Archangels
- Modernas
- Fantail
- Silver King

That's right, they are all fancy pigeons.

They should be kept in a wire netting enclosure from which they can see out, and fed with grain and dried peas.

All very nice, very cosy. But now it's getting practical again.

'Take squabs — young pigeons — from the nest to eat when the underside of the wing is fully feathered. Kill, pluck and cook them like little chickens. Silver King is a good breed if it is squabs that you want, but there is only a limited market for the sale of squabs and one gets rather sick of eating them.'

From *The Complete Guide to Country Living*, Suzanne Beedell & Barbara Hargreaves

Oh dear. Squab sickness. I think we'll go and look at flamingos instead.

Q **I would like to know if it is possible to keep flamingos in this country.**

A It is possible to keep flamingos in this country provided you have a pond between 12 and 18 inches deep in the centre, since flamingos spend 95 per cent of their time in the water. A hut must also be provided for winter, but it does not necessarily have to be heated. They eat ordinary poultry mash and will also take shrimps to keep their colour up. You will also find that it is better to keep four flamingos rather than two, as they like to be in a crowd.

From *A Guide to Country Living*, ed P.D.N. Earle

And absolutely no mention of eating them, although if flamingos catch on as pond ornaments it could be worrying news for shrimps.

A WHIM (SHORT LIVED)

I did once, for a challenge, start to breed lemmings, but the rabies scare soon put a stop to that.

From *Memoirs of a Ghillie*, Gregor MacKenzie

Really rural wildlife and increasingly desperate suggestions of how to prevent it

Sometimes our relationship with native wildlife is nurturing and harmonious. But other times it becomes a siege, with the embattled householder using every defence he can muster to keep back the encroaching hordes who want to share his home and garden. And yet the animals regularly come out on top. Perhaps it's better to relax, and let them in...

Jackdaws — Getting Rid of Them

Fix an alarm clock to the end of an 8ft pole, and set the alarm to go off at 3am and push it up the chimney. For those whose nerves will stand the strain of such an early shock, this seems a simple and practical solution.

From *A Guide to Country Living*, ed P.D.N. Earle

After some thought, sanity breaks through on this one:

Personally we've had a family of jackdaws nesting in one of our chimneys for years and they do no harm. We regard them as old friends.
Ibid.

HOW TO REMOVE COCKROACHES

As you do not like to use the powders sold to kill cockroaches, you must get a tame hedgehog.

From *Oh No Dear!*, Roy Hindle

Q I would be most grateful for advice on ridding my property of moles under the lawn.

A (1) Insert empty bottles base down into the runs – the wind noise across the neck of the bottle is supposed to drive them away.

A (2) Place small slices of lemon down holes about 6in to 8in deep in the lawn on grassed areas. If a grid of, say, 3ft square is made of holes over the lawn, this seems to have some effect. Disadvantage: lemons in bulk are expensive!

A (3) Having read somewhere that moles will not go within 70 ft of Caper Spurge*, and having been told by a friend that experience had led him to agree, I put in a few plants near the runs of my few moles.
(* Lathyrus, about 1s 6d a packet)

A (4) Moles can be kept at bay by planting a certain plant called Euphorbia.

A (5) I was very pleased to read your note on the subject of moles. I can give him the answer and that is to shoot them, and I am not joking.

From *A Guide to Country Living, ed P.D.N. Earle*

High Noon on British lawns! And here's the last word on the subject of mole eradication.

Euphorbia, Lathyrus and Caper Spurge are one and the same thing. Personally, I don't find it works. I have tried all these remedies and to encourage you, must admit that I have more moles in my lawn this year than I have ever had before.
Ibid.

Game, set and match to the moles, I think.

Batty

And finally, going right against the spirit of the time, here is a bat lover giving advice.

Q I have just discovered what appears to be a bat, clinging to the ridge board in the roof space of my house. Could you please advise me how to dispose of the creature, for while it has cleared all the spiders, the droppings are a nuisance.

A We would really advise you to leave the creature alone. It is commonly believed that bats not only keep spiders at bay but also wood-devouring beetles, and are therefore quite a valuable asset in one's roof. Surely one bat cannot create a great deal of droppings under the rafters, and if you were to spread newspapers underneath it would be very easy to dispose of any such droppings from time to time without too much trouble.

From *A Guide to Country Living, ed P.D.N. Earle*

Rabbity

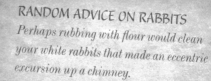

Modern research suggests that European rabbits originate from the Iberian peninsula. Following the logic displayed above, that would suggest that olives, garlic and asparagus would go down nicely. But I'd stick with hay, carrots and Happy Bunny food from your local pet shop.

Not recommended as pets

BADGERS

In the house, badgers are boisterous and mischievous and they do not make good house pets. They become too trusting and cannot be returned to the wild as they are vulnerable to both human and animal predators. They are not easy to house train, and do not always get on with dogs and cats. Badgers can bite very hard indeed and this also makes them unsuitable pets if they are to come into contact with strangers or children.

From *The Complete Guide to Country Living*, Suzanne Beedell & Barbara Hargreaves

Yes, I get the message loud and clear. Admire their stripy charm from afar. How about a beetle, then?

There are about 3,700 species of beetle in the British Isles, and not one of them is dangerous to man…

Sounding hopeful so far…

…*although several bite.*

Bother.

The ladybird can give a little nip and the green blister beetle may emit a substance which causes little skin blisters. The devil's coach horse, with its fearsome two-horned head, can also deliver a painful bite.

Not a green blister beetle then.

LET'S GO BIGGER, SHEEP?

Be warned that sheep suffer from various diseases and conditions which are all unpleasant, such as footrot, blowfly and liver fluke.

From *The Complete Guide to Country Living*,
—Suzanne Beedell & Barbara Hargreaves

PEACOCKS?

Peacocks are difficult birds to rear and keep, and can appear perfectly well one day and be dead the next. Peacocks roost on trees or walls, and do not take kindly, on the whole, to being shut up at night. This means that they are vulnerable to foxes; but are usually alert enough to avoid them. Unfortunately, the hens at breeding time become slightly dopey and it is then that they may be taken. Especially in the spring at breeding time, and at roosting time, the peacock lets out the most ear-splitting and heartrending cry, a kind of OOOOOOOOH on a rising and falling inflection. This tends to annoy the neighbours.

Ibid.

Mustn't annoy the neighbours. Something about an OOOOOOOOH on a rising and falling inflection brings visions of the Environmental Health Officer and his decibel meter.

WHAT ABOUT FOXES?

Orphan fox cubs are easy enough to rear, but unfortunately never become totally tame and must be released on maturity, so think twice before taking one on especially as foxes have a rank and lingering smell.
Ibid.

AND HERE IS SOME ADVICE ABOUT HEDGEHOGS

They should not do much damage in any garden, but they should not be allowed in the house, since as a rule they are swarming with fleas once let out of doors.
From *A Guide to Country Living*, ed P.D.N. Earle

So it's back
to a couple of
guinea-pigs
then.

Pet Pot Pourri

Five-year-old, reporting important event: 'The dairy cat has five kittens, three Friesians and two Jerseys.'
(Helpful note to the uninitiated: Friesian cows are black and white, and Jersey cows are marmalade. Which you probably knew anyway.)
From *The Countryman Animal Book*, B and M Campbell

INTRIGUING, AND SADLY UNFULFILLED ...
Instructions for making the nightingale will appear shortly.
From *Oh No Dear!*, Roy Hindle

They didn't. And I'd love to know.

PIGS
'Cats look down on you, dogs look up to you, but pigs is equal'.

Pets from the past

Here's a wonderful description of a pet-lover from the days when anything went and my great-grandmother had an emu living in her walled garden.

Theodore Hook went to visit Captain Frederick Marryat CBE FRS RN, the author of 'Children of the New Forest', who lived in a thatched house called Manor Cottage.

His first impressions were of the garden, which seems to have been zoological rather than botanical. As he approached the front door a brace of tame partridge got up. His host

then explained that Manor Cottage was also Liberty Hall: 'I open my bedroom window,' Marryat remarked, 'and jump out when I am dressed, which saves the trouble of unbarring doors.' Hook had no need to avoid walking on the grass. 'There were,' he recollected, 'animals everywhere: calves feeding on the lawn; ponies and a donkey under a clump of larches; a colt and its mama. There were coops of fowls standing on the gravel path in front of the dining room.' The children shared their father's love of animals: 'a jackdaw sat on the shoulder of one of the little girls, and as the party neared the lawn, it was joined by a number of pigeons.' But that was only part of the zoo: 'there were also an aviary, rabbits,

pheasant, partridges, cats, dogs and donkeys.'
The Captain moreover had seasoned his
crew with a nautical tang: 'In the walled
garden a tame sea-gull and a heron followed
them around.' Each member of the household
appeared to get on well with the others, for
Hook noticed that one of the Captain's
daughters 'seized and held a large rodent in
her bare hands, so fierce that it had killed a
ferret.' Captain Marryat would have shared
Joseph Addison's admission: 'I value my
garden more for being full of blackbirds than
of cherries.'

From *An Englishman's Home*, J.H.B. Peel

THE HEDGEHOG WHO OVERINDULGED

Tins or jars half filled with beer will catch a lot of slugs and snails; I leave them in strategic places until they are full. One night I noticed that tins which had been half full on my previous inspection were now empty. This happened several times and I was puzzled, until I saw a hedgehog leaning over a tin, disposing of slugs, snails and beer. Oblivious of my torch he kept at it and emptied the tin, then wiped his mouth with his front paws and moved off. His progress was unsteady, and after going some way he lay on his side and curled up. An hour later he was still sleeping it off.

From *The Countryman Animal Book*, B and M Campbell

IN

MEMORY

OF THE OLD FISH

UNDER THE SOIL

THE OLD FISH DO LIE

20 YEARS HE LIVED

AND THEN DID DIE

HE WAS SO TAME

YOU UNDERSTAND

HE WOULD COME AND

EAT OUT OF OUR HAND

DIED APRIL THE 20TH 1855

AGED 20 YEARS

Mourning a fish

AND A FISH MUCH MISSED

This memorial can be found by a stream at Blockley, Gloucestershire.

And finally...witherets:

We were looking for standing stones on the slopes of
Slieve Snaght in Donegal. The farmer, a man of about
forty, was welcoming and helpful. No, he had not
heard of standing stones thereabouts, but in
one of the fields there was a stone that had
caught the ploughshare so often that
his father had taken it up. They had
found an underground tunnel, and
his uncle had gone down with a torch.

'I'd be feart to go down there meself,' he
admitted. 'I'd be feart o' them witherets.
That's a class o' wee animal like a rat,
an' that's not got a bone in its body. Ye
meet one o' them witherets an' that'll put its
tail between its teeth an' whizzle at ye. I'm tellin'
no lie. That'll stay with ye for the rest of your days. Ay,
that's a wee kind o' beast like a stoat, ye know, an' there's never a bone till its body. I'd be feart to
meet them witherets.'

You have been warned. Should you chance to meet one, never hassle a witheret. Unless, that is, you
want to be followed around for the rest of your life by an animal that will put its tail between its
teeth and whizzle at you. Mysterious, but really rural.

REALLY RURAL
CHILDREN

REALLY RURAL
CHILDREN

Childhood hasn't always been a garden of delight. Not long ago, it was more in the nature of an assault course to toughen you up for adult life, whether you were being 'seen and not heard' in the manor house, feeding the pigs in the farmhouse or lace-making around the clock in a cottage. There was fun along the way: being a child it comes naturally. But it wasn't until you had successfully achieved adulthood that you could relax and gaze back benevolently at the past. From a safe distance.

The village school

Here comes **J.H.B Peel**, who left childhood behind him many years ago. He is viewing the remains of a village school through rose-tinted spectacles. And all looks rather nice.

The weather being perfect, and the afternoon still young, we made a short detour in search of Mainstone, following a lane beside the Unk, past the ruins of a handsome village school which, in years gone by, had taught the children all they needed to know. The three Rs, a smattering of history and Bible tales, the local flora and fauna, and the merits of belonging to a small community of farm folk.

Well possibly. Then again, it might have been more like this person's experience.

KNUCKLE RAPPING

When I was five I started attending the village school. The schoolmaster in charge of the older children was Mr Bearcock and I'll never forget him. A tall, stern, white-haired tyrant, we were all terrified of him because he used to cane us most mornings whether we deserved it or not – it was his way of starting the day. He lived in the schoolhouse with his niece, who also helped in the school sometimes. She was as bad as her uncle and frequently rapped our knuckles or pulled our hair.

From *Memoirs of a Fen Tiger,* Audrey James

The school bus

Even getting to school could be a trial. There are worse things than an overcrowded school bus.

My father was determined that we should be as tough as he. Today, most children get transport to school. My sister and I, for our five-mile trip, had a donkey – but only until I was five. Then he sold it: I was old enough to walk, whatever the weather.
From *Memoirs of a Ghillie*, Gregor MacKenzie

THE GOVERNESS
Alternatively you might have had a governess and been schooled at home. Here is a young gourmet's guide to schoolroom routine.

At 11 a.m. the footman used to bring up milk and biscuits on a tray, and at 12 we broke off and were taken out for a brisk walk with the dog along the road. After luncheon at 1 o'clock we lay on our backs on the floor for half an hour while we were read to and then we went out again for another walk or to play in the garden. Lessons began again at 3.30 p.m. and tea was at 5 round the schoolroom table, laid with a white cloth. We had a plate of cut bread-and-butter to start with and then slices from the loaf for jam, which was (sic) not allowed with butter.

akes, unless somebody had recently had a birthday, were of
rious plain varieties including those flavoured with the hated
raway seed. When these appeared we just went without cake
til the governess, who fortunately liked them, had finished.

om *The Private Life of a Country House*, Lesley Lewis

ke obviously mattered. After watching the governess gobble
wn a mound of rejects, the iron enters the writer's soul.

seems to me that what we received was not so much education as
quite useful substitute for it.

they had received a better grade of cake, the verdict might have been quite different. As it was,
e governess-raised children perceived the grass as being greener on the other side of the fence.

A LA CARTE

At 10 my mother went into the kitchen to confer with
the cook about the day's meals or, if it was Friday, those
for the weekend. In early days the list was written on
a slate with a slate pencil which, to my ears, squeaked
deliciously when I was allowed to use it. I envied the
schoolchildren who used slates habitually and indeed
admired them altogether for their supposedly greater
freedom and knowledge of the world.

Ibid.

Slates

Hmmm. Not sure everyone felt the same – let's see what Ernie James had to say about it.

The older children wrote in books but the young ones used slates. We all hated and dreaded sums, because the schoolmaster generally gave us a stroke with the cane for every sum we got wrong.
From *Memoirs of a Fen Tiger*, Audrey James

Not all village schools were hell-holes though.

My early days as a schoolboy were very happy times. We had a little village school in Wrentham and I walked to it and home again every weekday no matter what the weather. Even on my first day I went alone although I was only five years old. My parents must have reasoned that since I knew the way and no harm could come to me on the journey, there was no need for me to be accompanied. When I was ten, I went into the headmaster's class. He was a splendid man and when we left school we all carried away with us something of his remarkable character.
From *Gamekeeper*, John Foyster & Keith Proud

I get the impression that they would have happily swapped their slate pencils for a slice of cake, even the hated caraway seed cake, and all that went with it.

I'm still sticking with the footman, and milk and biscuits on a tray at 11am. As with so many things in childhood, both then and now, it was all in the luck of the draw.

Dear Mother, — I now write to tell thee we are all well. Benjamin is growing a pretty good boy. James doth desire a coat. Henry hath need of a coat also. Benjamin hath only one pair of britches. I would be obliged to thee to send him one. I would be obliged to thee to write to the Master not to let William be drinking the ink.

From *The Cottage Life Book*, ed. Fred Archer

The 1970s' classroom

Fast forward to the 1970s, and things have changed. Ronald Blythe can barely contain his astonishment at what he finds in the classroom when he goes to visit the village school.

The class-room atmosphere is transformed. The children are pretty and floppy. Maximum discipline has given way to casual expressionism. The indigenous village culture is overlaid with massive images from television and from advertising. But when the imagination does get working it really goes places, with none of the traditional taboos to check it.

From *The Countryman's Britain*, ed. Crispin Gill

So not all bad with the pretty, floppy children then. Mr Blythe went on to read them *The Jumblies* by Edward Lear.

'More!' they shout, where once their heads would have been splitting from the incantatory treadmill known as school.

From *The Jumblies*, Edward Lear

Childhood is all very well but there is much to be said for the established health, completed growth and unbroken skin of adult life.

From *The Private Life of a Country House* Lesley Lewis

Really Rural Today

THE RECEPTION CLASS TEACHER

It's the Free Play Activity at Appledew Primary School, and the children are being encouraged to extend their social skills through the medium of sticklebricks, dolls and the water-tray. Josh seizes the opportunity to construct a gun out of sticklebricks, and shoot up the Pretty Princess Fairyland Palace. Emily rises up in defence of the Palace and launches a counter-attack, using Pretty Princess Fairyland (currently dressed as a mermaid) as her weapon. Now Josh is crying because the mermaid tail shattered his sticklebrick gun. Meanwhile George who came to school dressed as Spiderman, has climbed up the Nature Table. On reaching the summit he treads on the dear little bird's nest (with eggs) that Ellie brought in that morning, and Ellie is crying because George has broken a dear little egg. Which smells distinctly suspect. Archie is looking strangely stiff and on investigation Mrs Evans finds that he is wearing a coat hanger inside his jumper. Daddy dressed him this morning because Mummy has gone to have a little baby sister in hospital.

Harriet and Matthew have made a supersonic mega speed launch pad that empowers them to throw all the plastic toys they can round up into the water tray from a great height. They soak Amy, who is passing, and Amy cries because her nice clean cardigan has a wet patch on it. Olive chooses this moment to announce proudly that she has had yet another Little Accident and the emergency knickers bag is empty. And the class still hasn't done the daily phonics lesson. Calling everybody to the carpet to sing through the alphabet, Mrs Evans reflects wearily that it is still five hours until Going Home Time.

Alice is 8 years old. She has been lace-making since she was five years old, first for five hours a day and now for ten hours a day. Lace-making school is held in a cottage room where 20 other pupils sit in cramped rows on stools with lace making pillows in front of them supported on pillow horses. Her arms and legs are bare so that they can be slapped easily by the lace mistress; her hair is tightly plaited to prevent stray hairs falling on the lace. She wears a stay busk to support her back while bending over her work, but her chest is already contracted. Apart from prayers said at the start of the day's work, education is non-existent. Life is hard for Alice.

D TODD

now...

Alice is 8 years old. She is in Year Three at school and doing nicely at literacy and numeracy. She is in the under 9s netball team. She enjoys school, and won the Merit Star for helpfulness last week. After school she does ballet on Mondays, swimming on Wednesdays and Gym Club on Fridays. On the other days she goes round to Mia's house, or Mia comes round to her house. At weekends the family often visits a Farm Park, because Alice loves animals and has two lop-eared rabbits. Soon it will be her Flower Fairy Birthday Party and Sleepover. She hopes that she will be given a pink nano iPod™. Life is good for Alice.

Following in father's footsteps

School's out! But as a rural child, once safely back home, you would probably find yourself a small but important part of the family business. Here are rural children learning on the job.

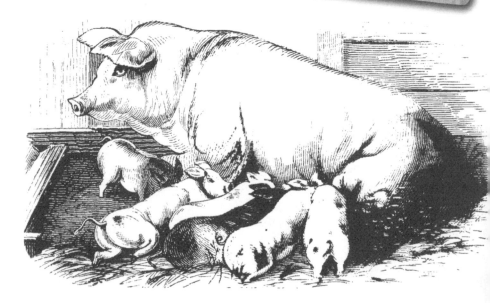

SMALLHOLDER

I always had jobs to do on my father's smallholding when school was over for the day. We kept about twenty pigs which we fattened up for market, and my first job on arriving home was to feed them. I used to go to the mangel heap, collect a bucket-load of mangels and clean them before feeding them to the pigs along with the pig swill.

From *Memoirs of a Fen Tiger*, Ernie James

GHILLIE

My brothers and sisters and I used to spend hours casting a fly at a half coconut upturned on the lawn. If we missed more than two or three times, we got the rough edge of (my father's) tongue.

From *Memoirs of a Ghillie*, Gregor Mackenzie

DRESSING UP IN AN ENORMOUS AMOUNT OF CLOTHES TO ENTERTAIN VISITORS

At 6pm, after nursery tea, we would be dressed up for a drawing-room session. I had a white dress of broderie anglais. (Under this went) combinations, a sleeveless bodice of quilted cotton to which suspenders were attached for black woollen stockings. Then there were white cotton drawers, very prickly, and a waist-length cream flannel petticoat...Over this was worn a stiff white cotton petticoat...My brother suffered perhaps more than me from starch, because he had to change his daytime striped sailor blouses to stiff white ones which had separate blue cuffs attached to the sleeves by links.

From *Private Life of a Country House*, Lesley Lewis

Nature's education

School never did agree with me, and I used to learn more on my way to school than I did when I got there. I liked to watch the birds on the rivers and in the hedgerows or wheeling about in the sky, and by observation I learned to identify them by their flight patterns. With other boys I played by the sides of the rivers, fished with homemade rods, and in the springtime collected frog spawn.

From *Memoirs of a Fen Tiger*, Audrey James

This is sounding better. Children tend to have a natural affinity with animals, and there are plenty to choose from in the countryside.

Mark, who was now aged five and a half, misinterpreted the reaction of the turkeys and took their frantic rushings at the wire fence to be a sign of affection. He spent many hours sitting on our side of the fence chatting away to one particular turkey that he named Esmeralda and could not be persuaded that her ruffled feathers and murderous onslaughts were anything but signs of affection for him.

From *Self-Deficiency*, Sally Borst

Children at war

Here are some young town evacuees getting to grips with rural life for the first time.

Four children yesterday playing in the cottage garden, happy and contented, and such different children from what they were on the night of their arrival. Already there was new colour in their cheeks. They hugged the dog, they hugged the cat, they ran forth into the orchard to get apples (permitted ones), and they dressed themselves up with greenery. The little girl made a skirt of mares-tails tied round her waist with a chain of fancy beads, and stood in smiling delight when I took her photograph. Then they were given baskets and sent off to get blackberries, which they did with cheery willingness. Everything was new to them, and all was lovely. For them the fields and hedges were a wonderland of joy.

From *War in the Countryside*, Sadie Ward

A definite improvement from this report, in tones of scandalized horror, on a different batch of evacuees.

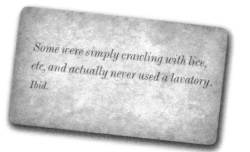

Some were simply crawling with lice, etc, and actually never used a lavatory. Ibid.

And here is an essay by an adolescent evacuee, beadily commenting on the new rural life she has been pitchforked into.

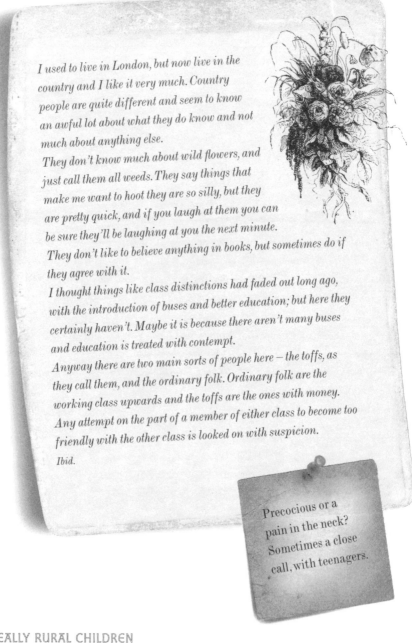

I used to live in London, but now live in the country and I like it very much. Country people are quite different and seem to know an awful lot about what they do know and not much about anything else.

They don't know much about wild flowers, and just call them all weeds. They say things that make me want to hoot they are so silly, but they are pretty quick, and if you laugh at them you can be sure they'll be laughing at you the next minute.

They don't like to believe anything in books, but sometimes do if they agree with it.

I thought things like class distinctions had faded out long ago, with the introduction of buses and better education; but here they certainly haven't. Maybe it is because there aren't many buses and education is treated with contempt.

Anyway there are two main sorts of people here – the toffs, as they call them, and the ordinary folk. Ordinary folk are the working class upwards and the toffs are the ones with money. Any attempt on the part of a member of either class to become too friendly with the other class is looked on with suspicion.

Ibid.

Precocious or a pain in the neck? Sometimes a close call, with teenagers.

Mealtimes

Sticking with the toffs versus ordinary folk scenario, here are a couple of descriptions of meals.

My mother was a marvellous cook. A great favourite of ours was a little beef pudding which was made in calico cloth. These puddings were like small dumplings to look at and they were delicious. Sometimes there would be an extra big one which I would scoop onto my plate. Inside there would be a turnip but no beef at all. Mother played a similar trick with the biggest sausage roll, inserting, instead of sausage meat, two clothes-pegs with just a little meat showing at the ends. Whenever I fell for these tricks of hers, everyone used to roar with laughter, including me.

From *Gamekeeper*, John Foyster & Keith Proud

Sounds like fun. Now off to the toff's dining room:

The usual weekday party was my mother, the governess and two or three children. Visitors had to put up with silent poker-faced witnesses, supposed to be seen and not heard, but who missed absolutely nothing. Some would feel constrained to bring the children into the conversation but we preferred to be ignored. We had our own troubles because we were under the eye of the butler and footman and this took some getting used to after the relaxed atmosphere of the nursery.

From *The Private Life of the Country House*, Lesley Lewis

THE NURSERY

Nursery meals were quite a battle. We seldom liked the food, picked at it and spilt it on the roughish chequered damask tablecloth. While we messed about it got cold and even more unattractive, in spite of being put on hot-water plates of blue and white china on a hollow metal base. The dinner and tea service started as a clean shiny white with bright blue and gold rim but it became discoloured and crazed from much use, and the plated cutlery, monogrammed N for nursery, was not polished and much dulled with time. Far the best meal was tea, especially in the winter when we made toast with the wire toasting-fork kept ready by the fire.

Not ideal either. At least, if dressed up to the nines and forced out for a formal drive, the silent poker-faced witnesses had the ultimate revenge.

MOTION SICKNESS

I suffered from acute travel sickness in any vehicle but an open trap. The drab cord material with which the interior was upholstered had a particularly nauseating smell and our other covered transport was little better from my point of view. It was a brougham, a one-horse carriage. I used to fix my eyes on the back buttons of the coachman's coat, seen through the little front window, as the waves of nausea rolled over me and sometimes broke.

Ibid,

Life before global warming

Leaving class distinctions well behind us, let us travel to the Fens and see what children did before the arrival of global warming.

When I was a young lad the winters seemed much colder than they do today and whenever there was a freeze up, crowds of people from miles around flocked to Welney for some skating. Skating was a very popular pastime in those days and nearly all the men and boys from our village owned a pair of skates. I was ten when I got my first pair, and they were wooden ones with turned up toes called 'Fen Runners'. Like all the other local children I taught myself to skate by pushing a chair along the ice in front of me.

From *Memoirs of a Fen Tiger,* Audrey James

IN AT THE DEEP END

Most of the children in Welney learned to swim when they were about five years old. It was essential to learn early with three rivers flowing through the village. The older boys swam in the Delph and when the younger ones went down to watch they were sometimes thrown in. It was the quickest way to learn how to swim but the older ones were always on hand to rescue any child who got into difficulties.

GOVERNESSES

So that was all right then. If you didn't have a Fen, but did have a governess, there was still plenty to do.

> *The governess let us bowl hoops, jump ditches, cut ourselves sticks, pretend to be horses and so forth, if we refrained from noisiness and deliberate mudlarking.*
> From *The Private Life of the Country House*, Lesley Lewis

NOISINESS AND DELIBERATE MUDLARKING

If you escaped from the governess, here are some outdoor games which could be worth a try: *The Wolf has gone to Devonsheer* which involved a lot of rushing about and yelling, or *Crocodile* with its memorable chorus of '*Farmer, farmer, may we cross your stinking, dirty, clarty water?*' (a North of England special), or *Puss in the Corner*.

PUSS IN THE CORNER

'Zest is needed to play this game. Too much caution in leaving the corners and the game falls exceedingly flat. A noble disregard for the danger of being cut off and it may be kept up for a long time.'

From *Games from an Edwardian Childhood*, Rosaleen Cooper

Awesome: let's do it!

THE GRASS IS GREENER

Then, noses pressed against the bars of the drive gates, the manor children gazed out and envied the perceived freedom of the village children.

They used to troop past in a spasmodic progress punctuated by bouts of the current game. It was either skipping, conkers, marbles, hoops, whipping-tops or hopscotch, which followed some mysterious cycle. We had hoops too, but we were only allowed wooden ones driven with a nicely turned stick instead of the much more exciting ones which ran through a hook, making a noise which children loved and grown-ups abominated.

From *The Private Life of the Country House*, Lesley Lewis

INDOOR GAMES

Indoor games were inevitably more sedate. Here are some classic drawing room games.

A papier-mâché box contained…the incomprehensible cards of some ancient game and a lot of beautiful mother-of-pearl counters. No-one understood the game. Other decorous games we played here, usually when there were visitors, were Happy Families, the Geography game which was a version of the former, and Wordmaking and Wordtaking.

From *The Private Life of the Country House*, Lesley Lewis

Anyone feel a sudden desire to go back to noisiness and deliberate mudlarking?

Whiling away the hours

In the gaps between school, chores and play, there were plenty of other ways of keeping children occupied, for example:

ORGAN BLOWING

Somewhere at the side or the back of the organ there would be a wooden lever, and beside it a hard wooden bench, at which the organ blower sat. Vigorous pumping would first be required to fill the bellows and after that it was a matter of keeping them full. Woe betide the organ blower who failed in that most vital — and least recognised — of the chapel's duties, so that the organ suddenly and embarrassingly died, waking some unfortunate lad from a moment's involuntary slumber.

From *The Country Chapel*, John Hibbs

OR CROW SCARING (REMEMBERED WITH LIMITED NOSTALGIA HERE)

The days when one could employ children armed with rattles, for a few pence, are long gone. (See also *Nuisances*.)

From *The Complete Guide to Country Living*, Suzanne Beedell and Barbara Hargreaves

OR MAKING MULE CHESTS

A mule chest provides a child with a workbench or seat of convenient height as well as a place for toys at the top and clothes at the bottom. A boy who is good at carpentry might set about making a mule chest for himself.

From *Furnishing a Country Cottage*, John Woodforde

OR COLLECTING GULLS' EGGS

First we would strip naked. We had to, firstly because we were liable to sink up to our chests in black, oily mud and secondly because of the plastering we got from the droppings of thousands of gulls wheeling overhead. We would take the eggs home and my mother pickled them in huge bread bins.

From *Memoirs of a Ghillie*, Gregor MacKenzie

If all else fails, how about sending them off to Lanark, to a *Whuppity Stourie*? This takes place on 1 March at the parish church. The bells are rung and the local children, armed with home-made weapons of paper balls on strings, pursue each other three times round the church, beating each other over the head as they go. That completed, the town officials, who have been watching the proceedings from the safety of a raised platform, throw down handfuls of pennies and the children all dive for what they can grab.

Now that's got to beat sitting in the bedroom playing a lonely game on your Nintendo™.

REALLY RURAL
HOME

REALLY RURAL HOME

The rural scene is dotted with homes of as many sizes and shapes as the rural people who live in them. It is all too tempting to fantasize about the picture postcard cottage, with its thatched roof, swallows at the eaves, roses around the door and Old Mr Sun smiling though the window. Or perhaps the manor house, grand yet benevolent, with many fine rooms and lengthy passages, all (in the mind's eye) sparklingly clean. Or a kindly, spreading farmhouse, warmed by an enormous inglenook fireplace. It is worth casting a glimpse backwards to see how the realities of living in these homes matched up to the nostalgic flights of fancy that have sold many a greetings card.

Reality vs rural Idyll

In *Furnishing a Country Cottage* a writer, known mysteriously as '**A P**', gives the 'perfect cottage' idea some clear-sighted consideration.

Owning a cottage must be the English town dweller's most cherished dream. His summer version has bees humming round hollyhocks and delphiniums in the garden, the scent of stocks and pinks drifting in through the open lattice. The winter edition has the roof crisply capped with snow, wood smoke curling from the chimney, and a warm fire glow glowing through the curtained windows.

Sounds wonderful. But focus in more closely. Could there be some ground-elder around the hollyhocks? Might a bee sting your nose while you were delightedly sniffing at your pinks? And are you the unfortunate soul who has to stumble through the snow to chop up the logs which will produce the pretty curling wood smoke (and incidentally prevent you and yours from being discovered frozen rigid by your lovely old oak settle)? 'A P' reckons this could be a distinct possibility.

Perhaps subconsciously [the English town dweller] skates over niggling memories of childhood stays in cottages…it is convenient to forget the coldness of the bedroom in winter, the icky, oil-smelling linoleum – and all that paraphernalia of cans of hot water in the morning.

ADVICE ON BUYING A COTTAGE

Most cottages look well at the time of year you bought yours, it is November, December, January and February in which they must really be judged. I have often said, Always buy a house in the winter.

From *The Countryman Cottage Life Book*, Fred Archer

Merits of a fire

Meet Mr Woodforde, who has been lovingly describing a former Hertfordshire gamekeeper's cottage that was a particular favourite of his, despite having no electricity or running water and whose sanitation consisted of 'a water closet containing a well-seated long hopper flushed by means of a pail of water standing by'.

WALLS

A quick study of the mud-pie school of architecture that created many of our cottages is also something of an eye-opener.

Walls were originally infilled with wattle and daub, or clay lump, or various mixtures of clay, earth, cow dung, horse hair, straw; anything which would make a waterproof and fast-setting fill.
From *The Complete Guide to Country Living,*
Suzanne Beedell and Barbara Hargreaves

So all that stood between you and the extremes of our maritime climate was a puddled mixture of earth and animal by-products.

This cottage is all right by Mr Woodford, and here he is singing the praises of quick action on the fire-building front.

It is true that the cottage strikes cold on returning to it in winter, but a great contrast is produced in a few minutes when wood and coal fires are alight. The wall opposite the sitting-room fire is near enough to absorb and throw back the warmth. One bitter winter's night I noticed, while listening to the proprietor playing a waltz on his harmonium, that the temperature was 88 degrees F.
From *Furnishing a Country Cottage,* John Woodforde

GREAT RESULT... but I suspect there was a long, cold interval before the logs, coal and frenzied harmonium playing finally got a fug up. And sooner or later you would have to leave the music and warmth and go out to discover the 'well-seated long hopper'.

Rural mod cons

Then there was the question of lighting. Pictures of cottages, particularly watercolours of cottages, often focus on tiny leaded window panes, crammed with geraniums in pots and tabby cats. Margery Fish came straight from a London flat to live in the country. She looked around such cottages and found them desperately gloomy.

When we first came to live in Somerset, just before the last war, every cottage window in the village was crammed with pot plants. In my ignorance I felt this was very wrong, and did not hesitate to say so. The rooms were very dark, with low ceilings, often made darker by beams, and the windows were always small. They were shrouded by curtains and then there were all the plants, packed close together and pushed as close to the window as possible to get all the light they could.

Mind you... the low ceilings and heavy beams would have the modern estate agent straining at the leash.

There were very few cottages of the old type left in the village, and those that remain have been modernized and brought into line with the bungalows, villas and council houses that are the people's choice today.
From *Cottage Garden Flowers,* Margery Fish

The great rural/urban swap

Given the choice between the chilly gloom of a picturesque cottage complete with long hopper, and a modern house with all conveniences, 'the people' let their feet do the talking and moved. As a counter-balance the rich man, who once could have been reliably found in his castle, or at least his manor house, started to modernize and happily inhabit the cottage that was formerly the sole domain of the poor man at his gate. What was the world coming to?

J.H.B. Peel in *An Englishman's Home* noted this 'topsy-turvy prospect' with every symptom of dismay:

The state of English cottage life during the second half of the twentieth century may justly be described as schizophrenic. On the one hand, farm workers despise a 'period' home, and prefer a council house with garage; on the other hand, businessmen and retired townspeople will pay more for a Georgian shepherd's hovel than the shepherd himself earned in a long and arduous life. So while old cottagers seek new houses, the urban immigrants outbid one another for the privilege of dining in the very room where their grandfather's coachman chewed cabbage and bacon. What a topsy-turvy prospect.

Topsy-turvy indeed.

Gracious living

The decision to chew your cabbage and bacon in a council house with garage could well be a no brainer. But why pay outrageous sums for the Georgian shepherd's hovel, when perhaps you had been used to a house such as Warley Side, childhood home of Leslie Lewis.

On the ground floor at Warley Side were drawing-room, dining-room, small passage-room, kitchen, pantry and, rather oddly, a large coach-house. Over the coach-house was a long room where the maids slept, as in a kind of dormitory, and round the side of the house were the stables.

From *The Private Life of a Country House*, Lesley Lewis

Plenty of room to breathe there. And plenty of useful rooms for cabbage and bacon chewing.

A rural rectory

Let's take a quick look at a description of a vicar's house in the days when 'The Old Rectory' came with rising damp and dry rot rather than a sense of gracious living and a massive price tag.

In 1895 the walls of Maperton Rectory in Somerset were so damp that moss grew inside the bedrooms. Few parsonages possessed a bathroom until the twentieth century. During the 1920s the bathroom at Whatfield Rectory in Suffolk was a wooden partition in the hall. Until the 1930s Radstock Rectory in Somerset lacked even a wash basin. In that same year the rector's wife at Beeston in Norfolk had to walk forty paces from the kitchen to the tap whenever she wished to fill the kettle. In 1955 the bathroom at Charlecombe Rectory in Somerset was an attic containing a twenty-gallon oil drum rigged above a paraffin stove; water had to be carried upstairs in buckets.

From *An Englishman's Home*, J.H.B. Peel

More mod cons

Size isn't always everything, and cottages can be cosier once they have had a bit of a make-over. And you don't have to carry the buckets so far either, a pleasant thought.

Let us hear again from an 'Old Hand', being cautiously pessimistic about an Evacuee's cottage but finally offering a tiny glimmer of hope.

Even if dear, [electric light] is clean, safe, labour-saving, convenient and pleasant. The best oil lamps are a great improvement on what we used to put up with, but lamp filling and trimming is a messy job. By the way, you have not mentioned sanitation. This like the water-supply and the heating of the cottage, has got to be right. If you don't have central heating there must be one or more perpetual-burning Esse anthracite stoves, with an Ideal or similar boiler for hot water, and – you will never regret it – an Aga or Esse cooker.

From *The Cottage Life Book*, Fred Archer

An Aga! Still the corner-stone of rural life in many a cottage, and manor house too. And on that happy note, it is time to visit some rural rooms, guided by contemporary handy hints gleaned from a rich variety of sources. Try them at your peril...!

The kitchen

The rural kitchen is the heart of the home and always has been. And now its décor is coming around full circle. In the early part of the last century it could well have featured flagstone floors, wooden dressers and old-fashioned ranges.

Shall we know again the days when wine and oil are plentiful, or have such glories gone, like the past, for ever? Much can be said in favour of modern kitchens. Will they degenerate into mere cubby-holes in which to heat the dull contents of tins, jars and cardboard boxes?

John Hampson, from *Country House Cookery from the West*, Elizabeth Lothian

...John was presumably standing in a hygienic marvel of vinyl and formica as he anxiously heated up a tin of soup on his shiny electric cooker.

A happy ending

The modern kitchens that concerned John Sampson (see page 121) reached a crescendo in the 1970s, epitomized by some DIY advice written by Mr Woodforde in 1972. Sensitive souls may need to look away now.

Very often it is more convenient to fit modern kitchen units in a small scullery-washroom alongside (traditional home of a great stone sink, to be put outside for a bird bath) and thereby gain a dining room and, perhaps, a degree of privacy while cooking.

From *Furnishing a Country Cottage* John Woodforde

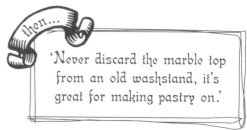

then...

'Never discard the marble top from an old washstand, it's great for making pastry on.'

From *1001 Country Household Hints*

now...

Why not insist on granite for the worktops in your beautiful new hand-built kitchen? It's great for making pastry on.

But John need not have worried, it all ends happily. Nowadays cooks tend to prefer company to privacy when cooking, and the soulless modern kitchens that concerned him are being stripped out and replaced by guess what? Flagstone floors, wooden dressers and old-fashioned ranges (think Aga). Wine and oil seem to be standing the test of time, too. Oh yes, and give the birds a proper bird bath, and bring back the old stone sink!

THE AGA LOVER

Emma's Aga has been installed, built on site by a specialist Aga-builder, and she is thrilled. She's been planning this moment for years, whilst doing business with a boring old electric cooker and now at last – here it is! Huge, block-shaped, re-enamelled in classic cream and radiating delicious heat even on the hottest summer day, the dogs are immediately drawn to it and sit around

admiringly in a hairy heap. Tilly, Emma's 10 year old daughter, is environmentally aware and doesn't approve of the Aga's yeti-sized carbon footprint. Emma says she'll plant a forest of fruit trees in the orchard to offset it but she will never, ever be parted from her Aga. She's been on a special course telling her how to cook with it, and dreams of starting an Aga-based catering business. She has a book of Aga handy hints, telling her how to dry herbs on it, and do her ironing with it. She has bought a set of table mats embellished with Aga cartoons. As she puts her first jacket potatoes into the roasting oven for lunch, Emma reflects happily that her life as a true countrywoman has really started, now the Aga has moved in.

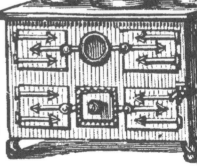

Other downstairs rooms

Leslie Lewis remembers her childhood drawing room as a tranquil haven of beauty.

Above the fireplace hung a big gilt mirror in the Chippendale taste but known to be a reproduction. The fire was fierce when made up for a party, and beside it stood two antique pole screens with oval shields. On the far side of the fireplace was a mahogany Georgian card table standing against the wall with its flap closed, and for games this would be moved into the middle of the room and opened out.

From *The Private Life of a Country House*

On the other hand, the parlour described by Ernie James, a 'Fen Tiger', is a simpler affair.

The room where the family lived was dominated by the fireplace which was flanked at each side by a cupboard. Standing in the centre of the room was an old, square table which was always covered by a dark-green fringed cloth. The only other items of furniture in that room were two Windsor chairs, a horse hair sofa which prickled the backs of your legs when you sat on it and a chest of drawers. Hanging on the wall was an old, square clock, Will's pride and joy, which he wound up each night without fail.

From *Memoirs of a Fen Tiger*, Audrey James

Beyond the parlour

And yet there are similarities – the fireplace, the table, the treasured furniture. But then the two descriptions dive off on different routes entirely.

Lesley Lewis muses that:

I can never remember raised voices or anything remotely sensational happening amid the soothing fragrance of flowers and furniture polish.

While our Fen Tiger notes happily that:

During the shooting season this room was usually packed full of birds which Will had shot.

Oh well. Both rooms were ideally suited to the families who used them. One thing they did have in common was a large open fire. Whether viewed over a toppling heap of dead snipe or from behind antique pole screens with oval shields, the life-giving heat of the fireplace reaches parts that a central heating radiator cannot even begin to touch.

Handy hot hints for the fireplace

Every rural home centered around the fireplace. A good blaze was life, warmth, cooking, and a cheerful blow struck against the long, cold winter. If not properly tended it could bring a whole new meaning to 'come home to a real fire', but that was a danger of which our forbears were keenly aware. Here are some fine, though potentially messy, ideas to keep your home fires burning.

• The old way to sweep a wide chimney over a wood fire was to drop one end of rope down it and tie a large bundle of holly twigs halfway along it. This should be big enough to be compressed by the chimney so that it will give it a good scrape as it is pulled through. Someone remains at the lower end of the rope to pull the bundle down again, and it should be worked up and down until the chimney is good and clean.

• Buckets of sand, kept in handy places, are a sensible fire precaution.
From *The Complete Guide to Country Living*, Suzanne Beedell and Barbara Hargreaves

For a really rural blaze, do as they did in Cornwall. Dried cow-dung or 'glaws' (Cornish gloas) was often used by the poor as a fuel. This was collected from the pasture fields during the summer evenings by women and children.
From *Cornwall and its People*, A K Hamilton Jenkins

Handy hints for those hard-to-reach places

Does time hang heavy on your hands? Is every surface in your home sparkling clean? But do you wake up at 2am and worry that you may have overlooked something? Now you can relax – here are some quick guide lines on how to seek and destroy the last tiny spots of grubbiness left in your home.

• Dip a pipe-cleaner in silver polish to remove tarnish from between the prongs of silver forks

• Reach those difficult corners in your freezer with towelling fixed over a pair of laundry tongs

From *1001 Country Household Hints*, Mary Rose Quigg

• Use a ball of crumpled silver foil from cigarette packets for cleaning the chrome parts of a bicycle

A heartfelt plea

Q Where might I obtain a well trained Butler?

A An Agency which trains them themselves is: Belgravia Bureau, 35 Brompton Road, London SW3.
From *A Guide to Country Living*, P.D.N. Earle

Tempting though it is to linger in the kitchen, and watch the well-trained butler scrubbing away at the spokes of a bike with the foil from a cigarette packet, there is more of the rural home to be explored.

The Bathroom

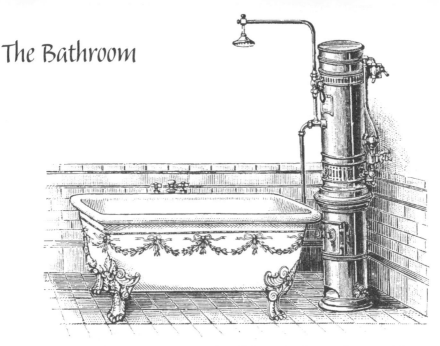

Here is Mr Woodforde again, not convinced that a bathroom is essential.

If finding space for a bathroom in a very small cottage presents an insuperable problem, then the answer is either to install a shower or make use of a tub. A Continental hip bath, which is on two levels so that you sit on a kind of step, is only 3ft 6in long and can be covered, taps and all, with a hinged lid. I once had one of these in the sitting room.

From *Furnishing a Country Cottage*, John Woodforde

What a great idea. Why not combine business with pleasure and host a tea party from the bath? Even if you take the plunge and decide to go for a bathroom, there are still pitfalls for the unwary.

There is no doubt at all that a bathroom and wc in one is a second-rate arrangement, and if a house or flat offers you this, ten to one it is badly planned throughout.

Mrs C. G. Tomrley needs a soothing sit-down and a nice cup of tea after viewing something this undesirable

Avoiding Social Shame

To avoid such an appalling combination as affronted Mrs C.G.Tomrley, any tiny space around the house should be hunted down and utilized. Mr Woodforde again.

A converted coal shed, wash-house or larder, though inconveniently distant from bedrooms, is easier to plumb than somewhere upstairs and has the advantage that it can double as a cloakroom.

Bidet

I feel that his heart is still with the 'hip bath in the sitting room' scenario. How does he feel about a bidet?

My list for a cottage bathroom includes no bidet…this cold and naked-looking appliance, offering a convenience to be secured by other means, seems at present a poor joke in an English country cottage.

No bidet then. And if you really insist on a bathroom, why not combine it with something that is actually useful?

PEARS' SOAP

A SPECIALTY FOR INFANTS

Perhaps, though, you can spare a room of reasonable size for your bathroom; if so it might be convenient to let it serve also as a dressing room, or as a laundry room that would keep the kitchen free of washing.

So what with one thing and another, I don't think a bathroom was top of Mr Woodforde's list of priorities.

COLGATE & CO'S CASHMERE BOUQUET TOILET SOAP.

A gentleman's ablutions

Now we are back in Leslie Lewis' house, watching with fascination as her father takes a bath. I feel certain that he was a man who would call for a bathroom of reasonable size and would heartily resent any attempts to double it up as a useful laundry space.

Like all the rooms in the house the bathroom was kept immaculately clean but if you had seen it just after my father had used it in the morning you would have got a shock, and the governess once nearly fainted. For washing he had a wooden bowl of soap about ten inches in diameter and a stiff brush made of vegetable bristles. He worked up a tremendous lather with which he covered himself all over and then, only then, did he get into the bath to remove it. The lather flew everywhere, often reaching the ceiling, and was a delicate pink if he had cut himself shaving, or spinach-green if he had been using a plaster for lumbago.

No wonder the governess nearly fainted. We will leave her drooping in the bathroom doorway and continue down the corridor to have a cautious look in the bedroom.

Handy hints for the home decorator

It may be that you own some quite large pieces and are anxious somehow to find a place for them. A grand piano will only find a niche where several rooms have been knocked into one large sitting room.

A carriage lamp may well in itself be decorative, having its parts ornamentally fashioned, but it was no more made for lighting a porch than horse brasses for drawing attention to the beam above an inglenook. Spinning wheels may be beautifully formed, but they were not meant to stand functionless in a cottage room. It's a matter of judgement.

There is a lot to be said for painting [floor] boards black; even the dullest-looking are transformed instantly at a cost of a few pence.

From *Furnishing a Country Cottage*, John Woodforde

Don't look now but something heavy is being wheeled into the Gun Room.

Go for it! A cannon in one end of the house, a grand piano in the other and an Aga in the middle. Who needs more? Now it is time to journey up the stairs and view the bathroom. Or possibly not.

The Gun Room

Q I have recently come into possession of an old cannon and wondered whether you could suggest anyone who could give me some information about it.

A We suggest you contact: The Master of the Armouries, The Tower of London, London EC3.

Handy hints for cleaning by interesting and unusual methods

• To remove cloudy marks off the inside of a decanter after it has been in use some time and has been emptied use stinging nettles head downwards in the decanter, which should be filled with water. Leave to soak and agitate occasionally until clean.

From *The Complete Guide to Country Living*, Suzanne Beedell and Barbara Hargreaves

• An ox-gall, to be obtained at a butcher's, will clean your carpet beautifully. The proportions are one-fourth of ox-gall to three-fourths of cold soft water. Apply to the carpet with a clean flannel, wrung out nearly dry from the mixture; do not make it too wet.

From *Oh No Dear!* Roy Hindle

• Soot on wallpaper – draw any surplus off with a cycle pump. Brush lightly with soft brush and rub residue marks with a soft rubber.

From *1001 Country Household Hints*, Mary Rose

Handy hints for dealing with laundry issues

• When children's white nylon socks have lost their freshness, boil them for a few minutes in water containing one or two teabags.

• Keep a pair of cut-off shirtsleeves in the car. If you have to lift the bonnet and tinker with the engine, you can slip these over your arms and keep your clothes clean.

• Tar may be removed by butter, and the butter by turpentine or French chalk, or by holding a red-hot poker near the grease.

From *1001 Country Household Hints*, Mary Rose

The Bedroom

Victorian advice on taste in the bedroom

Your Tudor bedstead, which you say has been already painted, might be made very handsome by means of good 'decorative panel painting'; but to paste pictures over it, in patchwork screen fashion, would be in very bad taste.

From *Oh No Dear!* Roy Hindle

A difficult bedroom inhabitant

An Ulster countrywoman describes the attire of her rheumaticky old mother, bedridden for sixteen years.

'Furst iv all she hess hurr flannenette shimee, then she hess hurr stockin's, then she hess hurr cambinations, then she hess hurr red flannen drawers, then she hess hurr corsets, lined wi' flannen, then she hess hurr nightgown on the top iv that, then she hess the blouse I gat made for hurr that's too tight in the armholes, then she hess hurr pattycoat, then she hess the black kerdigan I bought hurr, then she hess the new grey kerdigan our Willie bought hurr, then she hess hurr two wee shawls an'a skirt roun'hurr showlders an'annythin'else she kin gather up. Then she hess four feather pillas, a wee cooshion at this side an'an owl coat in a bunnel at the other side, hurr stick in bed wi'hurr an'a wee tin box she keeps hurr wee nigmanoys in. An'she lies there an'bombardeers us from the bed mornin', noon an'night.'

From *The Cottage Life Book*, Fred Archer

So there are worse things to be found in your bedroom than dodgy flock wallpaper. And on to the Spare Room, where a Guest is getting well dug in.

The Spare Room

We are back with Mr Woodforde, who is dealing with the delicate subject of looking after the Weekend Guest.

There is no arguing the proposition that a weekend visitor on average spends as many as eighteen hours in his bedroom. Indeed, his time there could be longer, even twenty-four hours, if he lingers over the breakfast and papers you bring him.

From *Furnishing a Country Cottage* John Woodforde

Twenty-four hours? In a weekend? What on earth is he doing?

Here is a list of props Mr Woodforde advises the caring host to obtain for the Guest.

Clearly a washing place of any kind should be supported by towels, soap, a carafe of drinking water and a glass, but you could improve on this by unobtrusively adding a bottle of aspirins, a pair of nail scissors, a comb, a bottle of disinfectant, and a tin of adhesive plasters.

A vase of flowers would be appreciated on arrival, but avoid too many ornamental items of china or glass which would be a source of embarrassment if broken. (Continued.)

Whatever is keeping the Guest feverishly busy in the spare room is obviously of a risky nature. And it might be advisable to duck if you enter his room unexpectedly.

Reading material

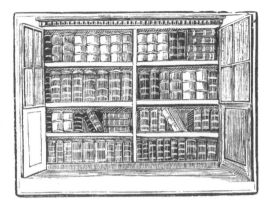

Advice follows on the kind of soothing pictures and reading material that would be guaranteed not to arouse the Guest while his host sought (for example) to remove the nail scissors that were probably a mistake to introduce in the first place.

Mr Woodforde's list goes on:

Edited diaries, works on the flora and fauna of the district, collections of essays or sermons. It doesn't matter if they are dull: starting to read a really dry book soon makes a person in a strange bed feel drowsy where an exciting, well written novel can have an effect which is the opposite of soporific.

Pictures should be fresh and bland; you can hardly go wrong with coloured prints of birds or flowers. A modern abstract painting which you admire yourself might have a perplexing, even an annoying effect on your guest.

And we really don't want that.

Leaving the Guest to hurl ornamental items at the bland spare room pictures, let us go back downstairs again. In fact, all the way down to the cellar, a good place to end this tour of inspection of the rural home.

The cellar

We are told that above all, a cellar must be dry. If there is some doubt about this it is time to visit the builder's merchant, don a boiler suit and prepare for an interesting wait.

Check that no underground drains are broken and leaking – bright green dye is specially sold by builder's merchants for this purpose. Pour this into each sink or bath in the house and into each lavatory (one at a time), flush away, wait a while and watch in the cellar to see what happens.

From *The Complete Guide to Country Living*, Suzanne Beedell and Barbara Hargreaves

Sitting down in the cellar and wondering whether at any moment a bright green fountain might start playing prettily in the middle of the floor would certainly hold the attention. However, if all goes well, and alien green does not come seeping out of the walls and ceiling, you will have somewhere nice and dry to use for all manner of things, such as a place:

...in which to store your homemade wine, to keep your enormous deep freeze, or to convert into a rumpus room or private disco for the kids.

From *The Complete Guide to Country Living*, Suzanne Beedell and Barbara Hargreaves

Stimulating ideas for other things to do in the cellar

And while the kids are having their private disco and the rumpus room is going full blast, why not squeeze in between the enormous chest freezer and the wine racks and have some 'me' time. Here are some ways you could while away the hours until the green dye comes seeping back through the walls again.

Shoe cleaning

The botanist H T Clifford, experimenting with mud scraped from modern footwear, succeeded in raising 43 different species of plant from a representative sample of shoes.

From *The Roadside Wildlife Book*, Richard Mabey

Useful plastic bowl making

If you take an empty half-gallon plastic orange juice container and carefully saw off its base, using a fine-tooth saw, you have made yourself a very fair cereal or soup bowl.

From *1001 Ways of Saving Money*, Tony Swindells

Rug making.

To make a hard-wearing and attractive rug for no cost whatsoever, you must first save old nylon stockings and tights over a long period. Cut them into strips. Knit, weave or crochet to the style of your choice.

From *1001 ways of saving money*, Tony Swindells

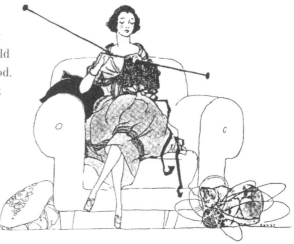

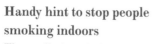

And finally...

Just before we bid farewell to the rural home, here is one final handy hint.

> **Handy hint to stop people smoking indoors**
> The smell of smoke is easily removed from a room by burning a few drops of vinegar on a shovel.
> From *1001 Country Household Hints*, Mary Rose Quigg

This should have them running for the exits.

REALLY RURAL
CRAFTS

REALLY RURAL CRAFTS

There was a time when the countryside reverberated with the merry sounds of a great many rural people being very busy. Thatchers thatched, millers milled, coopers coopered, harness-makers made harness and lace-makers made lace. Every village pulsated with industry. Then it all went strangely quiet and Asian sweat shops took up the baton. Now the pattern has changed once more and there is a growing demand for local, hand-made articles. Visit any country fair today and you will see hurdle-makers, hedge-layers, basket-weavers, spinners and the like, all hard at it and doing very nicely. Methods haven't changed much, and our forbears would recognise and applaud our current crop of rural craftsman. They would be pleasurably surprised by the prices that well-made produce can fetch, too. So should you wish to discover a bit more about rural crafts, both then and now, here is some freshly distilled rural wisdom to help you on your way.

Some rural activities you might like to pursue

MAKE A DEW-POND

Dew-ponds are a bit of a rural mystery – round ponds high up on chalk down-land which unfailingly provide water for thirsty sheep in the driest summer. If you would like to create your own reliable drought-proof watering solution, here's how to do it.

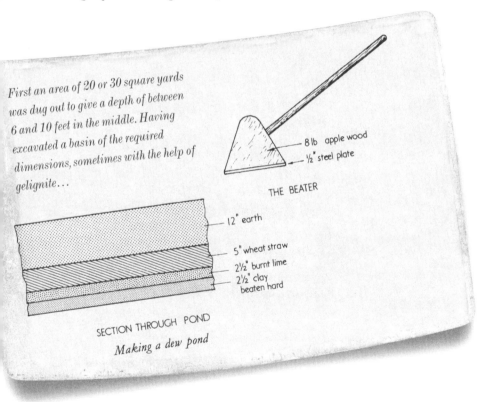

First an area of 20 or 30 square yards was dug out to give a depth of between 6 and 10 feet in the middle. Having excavated a basin of the required dimensions, sometimes with the help of gelignite…

8 lb apple wood
½" steel plate

THE BEATER

12" earth
5" wheat straw
2½" burnt lime
2½" clay beaten hard

SECTION THROUGH POND

Making a dew pond

Actually, on second thoughts, don't try this at home.

*It had to be lined with puddled clay to make it watertight…This was consolidated into an imperviou
layer of about 2½ inches by means of beating with a wooden mallet or beetle…*

(Can I put a quick word in for beetles here? They would prefer you to take the mallet option.)

*The clay bed of a dew pond was the most important feature and the expenditure of hard labour in
beating it solid accounted for most of the work. Having beaten the clay to a glassy smooth surface it w
covered with a 2-inch layer of lime which set the clay brick hard, making it impenetrable by worms.*
From *Crafts from the Countryside*, John L Jones

Doesn't that sound nice? Worm-proof and everything.

THE MERITS OF A DEW POND
In his 1937 trade card Mr Smith of Well Head, Dunstable, spoke proudly of his
'secret process…*handed down from father to son for 250 years'.* Mr Smith was also
a man who enjoyed a good long sentence.

*(Dew) ponds condense and retain their own water and are largely used for
watering horses, cattle and sheep etc but in recent years I have successfully applied
the process to Ornamental Water Construction whereby beautiful lakes can now
be obtained on any high or low or dry position whereby the pleasures of wild duck
shooting, boating, skating, swimming etc can now be enjoyed on the driest of sites
and has no equal as a water supply in case of fire, without the aid of pumping it.*
From *Country Crafts Today* J E Manners

So all it takes to make a dew pond is a ready supply of high explosives, several generations of
expertise and a great deal of hard graft. Perhaps it is time to consider something which is still a
touch mystical, but considerably simpler to achieve. If, that is, you are one of the fortunate few.

DOWSING

A dowser can pinpoint by extra-sensory means (not by witchcraft) all kinds of things, from water and mineral supplies to the causes of physical illness and the sex of chickens. Water diviners train themselves by experience and, although about 20 per cent of people have the ability to dowse, in only a few cases is it worth development.

Bend a couple of lengths of coat-hanger wire into L-shapes and hold one lightly in each hand. The movement over water is gentle but quite unmistakable.

From *The Complete Guide to Country Living*, Suzanne Beedell and Barbara Hargreaves

Who could resist? So park the broomstick, obtain a coat-hanger, and here we go. And the movement over chickens? It's worth rounding up a flock just to find out.

FLINT KNAPPING

Or would you like to make some gun flints for your flintlock gun? We are told that at the zenith of the profession, in the Napoleonic Wars, 200 flint knappers turned out 356,000 flints a month in Brandon in Norfolk to meet the army's requirements. Setting our sights lower, let us see how to turn out a small handful. Or even just one.

There is no secret about knapping. The process is straightforward, but a lot of skill and knowledge is needed to obtain a reasonable output…

From *Country Crafts Toda Y*, J.E. Manners

SQUARING
The flint is put on a pad on the left knee and struck in exactly the right place with a 4 pound hammer to obtain a square of about 6 inches. The square is put on the left leg and flakes are knocked off. These are about 4 inches long and 1 inch wide and naturally come off with a bevelled edge.
From *Country Crafts Today*, J.E. Manners

Yeah, right. It all sounds incredibly painful.

Craft miscellany

Gimping rapidly away from the flint knapping, let us try something softer. Such as:

BIKINI KNITTING.

This is more like it. Forget the beetles, and the wire and the 4 pound hammer, seize a pair of knitting needles and cast on lavishly for a DD cup.

The bikini knitters work to a high standard, producing garments of a specified design and using special, carefully chosen wool.

From *Crafts of the Highlands and Islands*
John Manners

Which is,
I like to
think, waterproof.

ULTIMATE MULTI-TASKING

Nothing is more common than to see the women trotting rapidly to market, with a most unconscionable load upon their heads, and with their hands, as if they were doing nothing else, actively and incessantly employed in knitting.

From *Cottage Industries*, Marjorie Filbee

GUESS THE RURAL CRAFTSMAN

Here we have four Craftsmen – A, B, C and D. See if you can guess which craft each is practising from an inspection of their tools, their clothes and their actions:

Q CRAFTSMAN A

Tools: adze, froe, pick, brace, bittle, bille

Clothes etc: tweed jacket, cloth hat, serious expression

Actions: he ties up bundles of timber with hazel 'ribbons'. Then he splits and weaves his wood around a hurdle-mound, with ten holes arranged in a slight curve.

Q CRAFTSMAN B

Tools: ligger, bottle of straw, leggett, sheep shears

Clothes etc: thick trousers, shirt with braces, cloth hat (worn sideways)

Actions: he ties successive bottles of straw to the battens with sway, then fastens swayed bottles to the rafters with iron hooks.

CRAFTSMAN C

Tools: draw-shave, riving iron (or flambard), centre bit, gimlet and wimble-wamble

Clothes etc: oilskins, boots, muddy leggings

Actions: he is mending his bar hurdles, which got a bashing in the breeding season. Then he will do dipping, or clipping. It is raining.

CRAFTSMAN D

Tools: steel leg-vice, floor-mandrel, swage-block, ball-peen

Clothes etc: leather apron, sweat

Actions: he is working in rhythm with his assistant, who wields a sledge. He is working on an ornamental gate at the moment, but he is also good at shoes.

HAVE YOU GUESSED WHAT THEY ARE YET?

CRAFTSMAN A is a wattle hurdle-maker

CRAFTSMAN B is a thatcher (the sheep shears were a ruse, to make you think he was a shepherd. But a thatcher uses sheep shears to trim the bottles of straw. Honestly.)

CRAFTSMAN C is a shepherd, doing some hurdling

CRAFTSMAN D is a blacksmith

Pitfalls for the unwary

It's a jungle out there, and counting the number of fingers left on a lifelong rural craftsman (out of a possible ten) can give you pause for thought. Here are some warnings, given by people who sound as if they know what they are talking about.

ALWAYS WORK A SLASHING HOOK AWAY FROM THE BODY, NOT TOWARDS IT.

SHARP TOOLS, OR THOSE WITH POINTS OR PRONGS, ARE PARTICULARLY DANGEROUS.

NEVER ADJUST ANY MOVING OR POWER DRIVEN MACHINERY WHILE THE ENGINE IS RUNNING. IT IS NOT SUFFICIENT TO PUT IT OUT OF GEAR. TURN THE ENGINE OFF

CAREFUL WHEN USING PARAFFIN
CHEER UP A SMOULDERING FIRE.
VER USE PETROL.

MANY PEOPLE HAVE DIED FROM A DRINK OF
PARAQUAT OUT OF A LEMON SQUASH BOTTLE.

Anybody feel like a spot of bikini
knitting instead?

IF YOU ARE CONTINUALLY
WORKING OUT OF DOORS AND
CUTTING YOURSELF, THEN HAVE
ROUTINE ANTI-TETANUS INJECTIONS.

All warnings from *The Complete Guide to
Country Living* by Suzanne Beedell and Barbara
Hargreaves.

Really Rural Today

A MODERN RURAL CRAFTSMAN: THE JACK OF ALL TRADES

Frank is a man of many parts. First and foremost, he is a gifted gravedigger, both for people and for pets. His proud boast is that nothing comes back up that he has put down, and he has to dig deep with badgers the way they are nowadays. The vicar respects him as a professional but wishes he wouldn't go on about badgers (also talented diggers) in the presence of grieving relatives. But graves are not all that Frank does. He can scientifically prune an apple tree to enormously increase its yield (and reproach its owners for years to come with the ghosts of unmade pots of chutney).

His bees produce beautiful golden pots of honey and candles that look as though they are made from earwax, but give off a clear and fragrant light. He's a useful man in the garden, except that to Frank a thistle is a thistle even if it's an ornamental thistle which cost an obscene amount at the garden centre. He will bury it deep in the compost heap at his first opportunity. Frank loves a good compost heap. He can try his hand at fencing with reasonable results, unless whatever is in the field really wants to escape. He had a brief, ill-starred attempt at laying paving slabs (don't talk to him about Her at the Old Rectory that had to have her patio re-laid three times before she was satisfied). And his attempt to put in some footings in at the Old Schoolhouse wasn't much better, although in his opinion the conservatory would have stayed up given half a chance. So what with one thing and another, Frank is happiest half way down a well-dug grave where he is a craftsman at the top of his game.

Frank knows where he is with a grave.

Falconry Furniture

**Ban any mental images of a tiny nest of tables
or upholstery with a fluttering songbird motif.
Falconers take their craft very seriously.**

*The equipment, correctly called furniture, consists of a
glove for the falconer and for the bird a hood, leash, swivel,
lure and bell. Every enthusiast needs a set of furniture.
The hoods can be most attractive and are made out of
leather of any kind and colour such as cowhide, lizard
or suede surmounted by a plume traditionally of herons'
feathers.*

*To make a hood the chosen material is cut to a pattern of
the required size and shape. It is hand stitched together
and wet-moulded over a wooden block to achieve the proper
shape. Finally the plume or thongs are added.*

From *Country Crafts Today*, J.E. Manners

Plume and thongs? This is kit for a fast bird!

A rural crafts quiz

TOOLS OF THE TRADE

Do you know your barley hummeler from your scud winder? If not I can tell you now that the first is a grid sort of thing for hummeling and the second is a handle sort of thing for winding, both very useful. To test your knowledge of simple rural crafting terms, here are some simple rural crafting questions, answers on the next page:

Q

1. How would you use a fagging hook? (be sensible)
2. Where would you hang a crotal bell? (be careful)
3. Where would you find a line of cleavage? (be serious)
4. Could you do a bobbin stitch? (be truthful)
5. Is there really such a thing as a scrolling iron? (discuss)
6. Why would you sing a waulking song? (be tuneful)
7. Where would you insert a drenching horn? (be gentle)
8. What do spelks, swills, scuttles, slops and wiskets have in common? (be brief)

A

Answers:

1. There are lots of uses for a fagging hook, which is a short-bladed sickle. For example, they are perfect for harvesting soft rushes, used for weaving.

2. You would hang it on a horse harness.

3. If you are about to make a cricket bat, procure a willow tree of about 15 years of age with a girth of about 50 inches. Take a length of the bole and cleave it with a large wooden wedge and mallet. An average tree gives about thirty-two clefts. The line of cleavage can be best seen from a diagram:

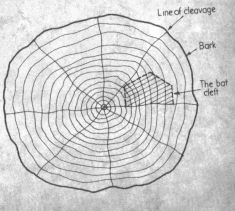

4. Well, could you? Check your answer against the expert's:

To make a stitch take two pairs of bobbins and carry out the following sequence of movements:

- *Take the two middle bobbins and put the left over the right,*
- *Take the two outside bobbins and put right over left,*
- *Cross the middle ones,*
- *Twist the two outside ones over three times.*

This operation makes one complete stitch. Then you continue with your lace-making, using anything from 30 to 100 bobbins depending on the width of the pattern, remembering at all times that mistakes show up badly and have to be rectified with a lot of unwinding.

From *Country Crafts Today*, J.E. Manners

5. There certainly is! A blacksmith would use one for decorative forged ironwork.

6. Probably to divert your mind from the sheer horror of saturating a piece of cloth with ammonia, warm water and soapsuds and working it vigorously to finish it. Another word for waulking was fulling, and don't even ask where the ammonia came from.

7. In the mouth of a horse. With stomach-ache. Rather you than me.

8. Of course you're right – they're all names for spale baskets*!

* spale baskets. A rather different basket which was once widely used, particularly in the north of England, made by interweaving lengths of thinly cleft oak. But you knew that already.

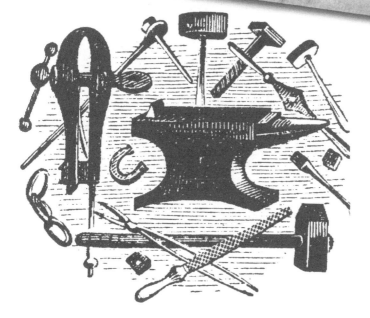

The perils of thatching

Imagine that you have bought a pretty cottage. It has an inviting porch, attractive casement windows and a lavender-lined path leading to a little wicket gate over which you can greet your new neighbours. All this idyllic property needs for perfection is a new roof. How about thatch? After all, you have done your homework and discovered that:

Although for a time thatching was a dying art, it is now flourishing, and there are plenty of thatchers working, although they are all fully occupied and you will have to take your place in a queue for their services...

From *Country Crafts Today*, J.E. Manners

No problem with supply, then, even if you have to wait a while. But what you have not taken into account is the alarm bells that seem to ring every time a finished piece of the thatcher's art is contemplated. The danger is...

FIRE!

At first the panic is hidden beneath a thin veneer of reassurance.

Fire danger is not really very great. In the old days, people kept long hooks with which to drag burning thatch off roofs, and, as oak roof timbers were slow to catch fire, there was usually more mess than damage and a new thatch set things to rights. The sensible precaution is to have fire extinguishers handy, a hose which can throw water onto the roof and a long ladder. If the roof timbers will support it, asbestos sheeting, fixed on the inside of a thatched roof, will externalise any fire from chimney sparks, lightning or bonfires.

From *The Complete Guide to Country Living* by Suzanne Beedell and Barbara Hargreaves

So no problem as long as you've got some long hooks, fire extinguishers, ladders and an extreme hosepipe. Not very reassuring really, and do I need to stress that the asbestos idea would now be frowned on by just about everybody? Most thatch seems to survive unburned anyway, which could have something to do with the long, wet British summer.

The village blacksmith (a case study)

We will move on from the hazards of fire to a man who positively embraces the stuff. It is central to his craft.

> Under a spreading chestnut tree
> The village smithy stands;
> The smith, a mighty man is he,
> With large and sinewy hands;

There is no doubt that Longfellow's poem was excellent PR for the blacksmith, but then he deserved it. Nowadays he probably specialises either in blacksmithing (working with iron) or farriery (shoeing horses), but until recently he tended to do both. He could also be called on to do haircutting, dentistry, car repair, knife sharpening, welding, horse doctoring and if he lived in Gretna Green, wedding ceremonies. Today a blacksmith can usually turn out a pretty good ornamental weathercock too. What a great guy!

Or, of couse, girl.

The widow of Walter Greenhough of Childrey, Berkshire described how she worked alongside her husband in the forge.

When his chance came for a forge of his own, he found himself stuck for a striker — for he had no money to pay for one. I said to him, 'You've always wanted to go on your own. Try me! I'm your man.' He gave a little start, flung out his right arm and with his eyes all a'glisten, said, 'Girl, you shall try your hand.' He did the smithing and me the sledging. I trembled lest I might hit his head and not the anvil the first day we worked together...beating out and welding a roadman's pick.'

From *The Village Blacksmith*, Ronald Webber

ESSENTIAL TO THE JOB
In fact fire and its effect on iron is what a blacksmith is all about, whether he is making a decorative gate, shoeing a horse or welding a roadman's pick with the help of his wife. As he warms up his forge, he plays on the bellows, breeze and fuel as if on a stringed instrument to get the optimum temperature for his work.

All this and a sense of humour too. (See overleaf.)

There is a story about Coleridge stopping at a Somerset smithy to have a shoe replaced on his horse. While there, he asked the blacksmith the time. The blacksmith bent down, lifted up one of the horse's hind legs and, seeming to gaze fixedly at it, said, 'Half-past eleven.' Coleridge was naturally astonished and asked the blacksmith how he knew so accurately by inspecting the leg of a horse. The blacksmith replied with a smile, 'Do you think, sir, that I have shod horses all my life and don't know by the sign what the time is?'

Coleridge puzzled over the matter for some time but could think of no explanation, so finally he asked for one. The smith smiled again and replied, 'Come here, sir. Now stoop down and look past the horse's hind leg to that pollarded oak yonder.' Coleridge did so. Through a gap in the branches of the oak tree the church clock was plainly visible.

From *The Village Blacksmith*, Ronald Webber

How they all laughed.

Inuits vs blacksmiths

Inuits are famed for the wide variety of names they apply to snow but they have nothing on the blacksmith in his smithy when describing his craft. Here are some of the printable names he gives to the metal on his anvil, as it changes colour in the heat.

FARRIERS OF NORWICH
NORFOLK BLACKSMITHS

15 February 1902

M B. Fernwick

	s	d
Osforarfada	2	0
Afortheos	1	0
Ashuinonim	2	0
Anafechinonimagin	1	0
	6	0

The names given to these heats are 'warm' when the heated iron is just not hot enough to glow in shadow, and 'black' when it glows very faintly; and these are followed in order by such heats as cherry-red, dull-red, blood-red, bright-red, and bright-yellow. Other heats (for welding) have names like snow-ball, full, light, slippery, greasy and sweating.

A Norfolk blacksmith sent the following bill to a customer.

Which being translated from the Norfolk dialect reads: horse for half a day; hay for the horse; a-shoeing of him; and a-fetching of him again.

You didn't get rich by being a blacksmith, either.

Another rural crafts quiz

THE RIGHT WOOD

You are strolling down a hedgerow, gazing at what Wordsworth described as *'little lines of sportive wood run wild.'* Our forbears tested and refined the trees and shrubs of the sportive wood, discovering along the way that (for example) ash trees have 'noxious drip', the wych-elm does not sucker, holly berries taken in large numbers are an emetic and spindle leaves smell horrible if crushed. See if you can guess what wood you could gather from hedge trees and use to make the following items. That is if you were impervious to weather, naturally good with your hands and prepared to practise for the rest of your life:

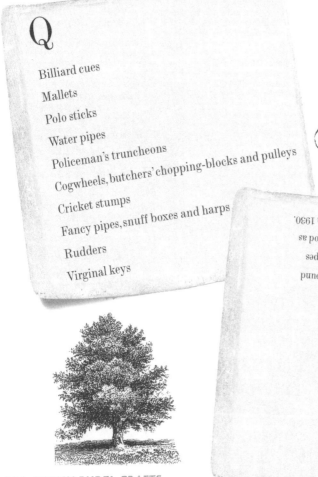

Q

Billiard cues

Mallets

Polo sticks

Water pipes

Policeman's truncheons

Cogwheels, butchers' chopping-blocks and pulleys

Cricket stumps

Fancy pipes, snuff boxes and harps

Rudders

Virginal keys

*straight trunks and branches put underground in London for water pipes in 1613 were still 'as good as new' when uncovered in 1930.

...ndle

...old Maple

...ornbeam

...sh

...lm *

...sh

...rabapple

...sh

A

Useful wood, ash. As an added bonus, Yorkshire girls believed that if they tucked an ash leaf under their pillow and recited the following poem:

Even-ash, even-ash
I pluck thee,
This night my true
love to see.
Neither in his rick
nor in his rare,
But in the clothes he
everyday wear.

A vision of their future husband would appear as if by magic. Although it does seem an opportunity missed that he would appear in his boring old work clothes rather than in his rick or (particularly) his rare.

DOES BELL-RINGING APPEAL?
BELL-RINGING. A PASTIME ENJOYED BY ITS DEVOTEES, BUT NOT ON THE WHOLE BY THE UNINITIATED GENERAL PUBLIC FOR WHOM THE CHANGES BEING RUNG ARE A MEANINGLESS RACKET. TO LIVE NEAR A CHURCH WITH AN ENTHUSIASTIC TEAM OF AMATEUR BELL-RINGERS CAN BE TORTURE. HOWEVER, IF IT APPEALS TO YOU, APPROACH YOUR LOCAL VICAR, WHO WILL INTRODUCE YOU TO WHOMEVER IS IN CHARGE. YOU CAN'T BEAT THEM, SO JOIN THEM! MANY WOMEN ENJOY BELL-RINGING.

From *The Complete Guide to Country Living* by Suzanne Beedell and Barbara Hargreaves

Ding dong!

REALLY RURAL
OUTDOORS

REALLY RURAL
OUTDOORS

The British Isles are admittedly compact, but somehow they contain a vast amount of rural outdoors. So how about growing some onions in it? Or some flowers? Or, for that matter, building a ha-ha? You might like to go for a jolly, healthy walk, or combine bird watching with a nice drive in the country. Or do the impossible and pitch a frame tent. It's all out there and waiting for you, and so are the rural types who have long been doing all of this and more with passion, verve and the dogged determination in the face of adverse weather conditions that is a prized part of our national character. There's so much to do in the rural outdoors and your only limitation will be your attitude to rain. Let's start with gardens.

The formal garden

Would topiary and a ha-ha be to your taste? Would you be prepared to chase the rams off your tennis court? And (the ultimate test) could you grit your teeth and keep smiling when the uninitiated tried to compliment your beautiful garden and then got it hideously wrong? Yes? Then look no further. Here is a formal introduction to the really rural garden.

ADVERTISEMENT FOR TOPIARY, BY ALEXANDER POPE (yes, the Alexander Pope)

* * *

ADVERTISEMENT

GARDEN TOPIARY

ST GEORGE in Box; his Arm scarce long enough, but will be in a condition to stick the Dragon by next April.

A green dragon of the same, with a Tail of Ground-Ivy for the present.
NB These two not to be Sold separately.

A Quick-set Hog shot up into a Porcupine, by its being forgot a Week in rainy Weather.

Adam and Eve in Yew: Adam a little shatter'd by the fall of the Tree of Knowledge in the great storm; Eve and the Serpent very flourishing.

The Tower of Babel not yet finished.

* * *

Once the topiary is in place, and St George's arm is long enough to stick the dragon, what next? A grass tennis court, of course.

From *Curious Britain*, Anthony Burton

Q As I was not going to use my grass tennis court last year I kept a couple of rams on it in the early summer. The result was a thick mass of grass in the autumn, almost comparable to a coir doormat. As I want to use the court this year I tried to cut it, but nothing could compete. I have a flame gun. Should I burn it off with this?

A We certainly think that a flame gun may be effective.

From *A Guide to Country Living*, P.D.N. Earle

Of course it would be. Toast the rams. And then on to the next logical step.

Q I want to build a ha-ha between the bottom of my garden and the beginning of the park to replace some unsightly railings and I would be glad of your advice on this matter…

A The usual depth is 5 ft and the distance across the top 9 ft and the width at the bottom 4 ft. The bottom should be given a 'fall' so that the water can get away.

Ibid.

Planting

So now you've got a forest fire and an enormous hole with a waterfall. Time for some serious planting and then you can show off the glories of your formal garden. But first prepare yourself mentally for the well-intentioned few who just don't get it, as described by **Margery Fish** in *Cottage Garden Flowers.*

The late Mrs Clive told me once how a very ignorant visitor had been taken round her fabulous garden but of course found very few plants in it that were known to her. She wanted to pay a compliment on parting but not knowing the name of anything made it rather difficult. All she could find to say was, 'You do grow wonderful dandelions,' much to Mrs Clive's amusement.

From *Cottage Garden Flowers*, Margery Fish

Oh well.

And now, leaving the roar of the flame gun and the clink of the spade (as the under-gardener opens up a cavity between the bottom of the garden and the beginning of the park) behind us, let us stroll on to a gentler option.

The cottage garden

RURAL NAMES FOR COTTAGE-GARDEN PLANTS, JUST TO ENJOY.

Hose-in-hose (primrose)
Jack-in-the-green (another primrose)
Jack-in-the-pulpit (wild arum)
Jackanapes-on-horseback (daisy)
Grim the Collier (hawkweed)
Bloody Butcher (lungwort)
Ploughman's Mignonette (creeping euphorbia)
Bridget-in-her-bravery (rose campion)
Bastard Balm (mint)

Bonding with your garden

Now we meet **Margery Fish**, the doyenne of cottage gardens. Her garden is not just an attractive place in which to erect a deckchair. She sees her plants as a much-loved though dysfunctional family:

(Margery) had Cyclamen hiemale, vernum, atkinsii and coum, with ibericum, only to find their seedlings totally indistinguishable; when showing visitors round the garden in January she referred t[o] them as her unlawful children.

From *Margery Fish's Country Gardening*, Timothy Clark

'Omphalodes verna is really an April flowerer but it usually cannot wait till then. I often see a little blue eye looking up at me in really wintry February weather when all good children should be asleep.'

From *Cottage Garden Flowers*, Margery Fish

PERSONALITY

Every flower is known intimately and has a personality to assert.

Pulmonaria officinalis: icy and aloof

'Queen of Spain' daffodil: *a frightened lady*

Horsfieldii daffodil: *a man with shrugged shoulders and collar turned up, trying to avoid the rain*

Campion: *gay, artless and good tempered*

Pheasant's Eye narcissus: *an old friend*

Old Bloody Warrior wallflower: *a difficult and dessicated old gentleman*

Ibid.

Sometimes the plants club together and do something useful.

Two other plants included for entertaining visitors were Hacquetia epipactis and Liriope muscari.

What bliss to be able to potter off and have a cup of tea while the *epipactis* and *muscari* got on with the business of showing the visitors around the place.

t wasn't all joy though, the relationship had its dark side.

The golden-yellow helodoxa *was more difficult to please, and Margery was always unhappy when a ifficult plant defeated her.*
rom *Margery Fish's Country Gardening,* Timothy Clark

And then...

(Cerastium) crept in through the hedge from the cottage next door, and having once got a foothold it proceeded to entrench itself firmly in a place where I could not dislodge it...A wall has now taken the place of the hedge but that will not help me now. The enemy is within the gates and will infiltrate my domain.

From *Cottage Garden Flowers*, Margery Fish

This garden seems to have got above itself.

THE SMELL OF HONEYSUCKLE IN THE MORNING ...

West-country landlady to prospective tenant who had admired her fine honeysuckle bush:'Ah, but you should see it in the summer-time, Mrs Brown; the stench fairly ruptures you.'

From *The Countryman Book of Humour,* ed. Margaret Cambell

Really Rural Today

THE MODERN
(HOPELESS) COTTAGE GARDENER

Lizzie is the despair of her gardening friends. It's not that
she's got the proverbial brown thumb; on the contrary,
everything she plants springs into exuberant life. But she
has no idea how to plan and order her flower beds. Not
for Lizzie the pruning, mulching, digging and splitting
activities practiced in more disciplined gardens. Lizzie
finds that she can't prune (it seems such a shame after the
plant has tried so hard to grow) and she isn't much good
at weeding either. Removing a seedling because it might
be a weed seems like an underhand act when it might
grow into something lovely, like the delightful variegated
ground-elder she discovered the other day. As a result,
dandelions, cow-parsley and bindweed (such a pretty
pink and white flower) bloom proudly in her herbaceous
border alongside the delphiniums, geraniums and peonies
that were the original inhabitants. Meanwhile her
lawn, under the same benevolent regime, looks
remarkably similar to the beds.

When a serious gardening friend comes to 'give Lizzie a hand', armed with secateurs and pruning shears, Lizzie finds herself protectively spread-eagled in front of her favourite shrubs which are rapidly growing to the size of forest trees. Later on, recovering on the wooden bench in what used to be a croquet lawn and is now a wildflower meadow (very ecologically sound), Lizzie listens contentedly to the buzz of neighbours' lawnmowers at work on stretches of bright green velvet. She has just discovered that rose-bay willow-herb, normally considered a weed although she has a fine clump of them right by her house, was originally imported from America as a garden flower. She feels vindicated.

THE NATURALIZED GARDEN

When I pass a house newly erected in a meadow, and see the zealous owner in his shirtsleeves, with stakes and measuring line and spade, starting to make a garden, I want to plead with him, 'Don't do it. You are destroying that heaven-set gift, Nature's garden, which is at your door. In return you are dooming yourself to hours of recurrent back-aching toil with fork and hoe. To revert to a native sward and a native hedgerow, to daisied lawns and dog roses, needs a husbandly effort. Then when you have obtained your field again, with orchard trees in it, you can look a dandelion in the eye and feel jolly, which you never could before you banished the word weed from your vocabulary.

From *Suffolk Harvest*, Adrian Bell

And here is another writer, trigger finger on the strimmer, itching to take a firm line with his garden.

The sort of garden I have in mind is secluded and mostly green... its only border is a row of herbs by the kitchen door: it is both outdoor room and an extension of the countryside. The garden has few boastful blooms to prevent it blending with neighbouring fields and woods: it is just a plot surrounded by a stout thorn hedge and containing hardly anything but grass, a few old apple trees and perhaps a quince.

From *Furnishing a Country Cottage*, John Woodforde

So dig out the flame gun again, torch the boastful blooms, and relax. Don't even worry about keeping the lawn stripey.

..there is something very satisfactory about leaving part of the grass uncut...
Ibid.

Very, very satisfactory. Farewell the Queen of Spain, and (particularly) farewell the Old Bloody Warrior. Beat back the enemy within the gates, and enjoy the peace.

In such a garden you can sit at ease and drink your wine.
Ibid.

And, of course, look a dandelion in the eye again, and feel jolly.

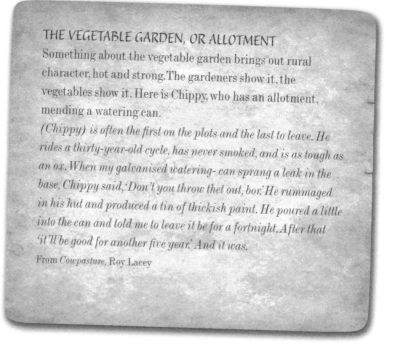

THE VEGETABLE GARDEN, OR ALLOTMENT

Something about the vegetable garden brings out rural character, hot and strong. The gardeners show it, the vegetables show it. Here is Chippy, who has an allotment, mending a watering can.

(Chippy) is often the first on the plots and the last to leave. He rides a thirty-year-old cycle, has never smoked, and is as tough as an ox. When my galvanised watering- can sprang a leak in the base, Chippy said, 'Don't you throw thet out, bor.' He rummaged in his hut and produced a tin of thickish paint. He poured a little into the can and told me to leave it be for a fortnight. After that 'it'll be good for another five year.' And it was.

From *Cowpasture*, Roy Lacey

One in the eye for the throw-away society. Then we have Rummy, who liked strong onions.

Rummy says we have lost the taste for onions. When he was a backus boy – back of the farmhouse – at Kirton, the farmworker's midday meal was a hunk of bread with a wedge of cheese and a home-grown onion. 'That were a strong 'un, bor,' he said 'a few bites of that and you could shut a five-barred gate at fifty yards. Now no-one wants an onion that answers back.'
Ibid.

Despite the note of nostalgia, I am quietly thankful that onion-breath that could shut gates at fifty yards is now a thing of the past.

THE HONEST POTATO

The vegetables didn't have it all their own way though. Here are aspersions being cast at the honest potato.

Potatoes have come a long way since they were introduced to this country by Sir Walter Raleight. The potato took time to be accepted in Europe because – wait for it! – once again this vegetable was supposed to be an aphrodisiac! (a potato an aphrodisiac? I don't believe it!)

From *Country Cottage Companion*, Peggy Cole

I suddenly want to take up arms for the potato, and hint at the strong appeal of the crinkle-cut chip.

Let's leave the potato, smouldering away in croquette form and study ageism instead, which seems to be rife in the vegetable patch.

AGEISM

It should be easy to keep an eye on the garden to avoid that wasteful tragedy, the too-well-matured vegetable. A broad bean kept till its green jerkin has turned to a fawn spongebag is a broad bean misunderstood. Bullet-like peas, long, tough, hairy runner beans, harvest-festival marrows — those who live in towns or placate a gardener must put up with these; but the cottage cook, if she grows her own vegetables, need not submit to such odious longevities. She must pounce on the innocents; nature will always see to it that there are enough sexagenarians.

From *The Countryman Cottage Life Book*, Fred Archer

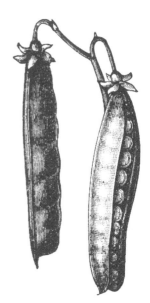

It all seems rather brutal, somehow. And while we are on the subject of brutal, just see what the creation of a really good compost heap can do to the finer feelings.

NURTURING THE COMPOST HEAP: THE PRACTICAL SCHOOL OF GARDENING

(Margery) became an addict to the compost heap. Everything suitable, from newspapers to straw bales to egg shells and tea leaves, went into it. She was lucky in having loyal help from Jean Gascombe and Maureen Whitty in the garden. She had been out lecturing and on her return was told that Jean's nose had been profusely bleeding. 'But what did you do with the blood?' asked Margery. 'Put it on the compost heap I hope.'

From *Margery Fish's Country Gardening*, Timothy Clark

Um, we are talking farmyard manure here, chaps, aren't we..?

Short rural quiz

Q

Study these names:

Black Norman
Breakwell Foxwhelp
Strawberry Norman
Barn Door
Slack-ma-Girdle
Fair Maid of Devon

In your opinion are they:

(a)   A gang of well-known West Country thugs
(b)   A band of well-known Morris dancers
(c)   Varieties of cider apple

A

The answer is (c), but it's a sham really. I would prefer them to be the West Country thugs: Strawberry Norman, terror of the cream-tea shops. Or Slack-ma-Girdle, lynchpin of the Merry Morris Dancers.

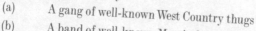

Pests and predators

We love our fruit and vegetables, and so do a lot of other things. Many pages have been written on fighting off the intruders, by fair means or foul. Here, for example, are carefully studied ways of avoiding bird damage to fruit.

Method	Comments
Automatic bird scarer	*Creates bad feeling among neighbours without fruit who prefer peace and quiet.*
Pulling old stockings over branches of cherries	*It looks most odd.*
A blast or two with a shotgun	*Most effective but again it upsets bird lovers.*
Cats	*The only sure-fire way to get rid of bullfinches.*
Children	*They come a bit pricey these days.*
Dogs	*Train him to chase birds, he will get rid of them without killing them, but of course may himself do damage to plants.*
Hawk-shaped kites	*Cannot be flown for long without attention except in very steady weather.*

From *The Complete Guide to Country Living*, Suzanne Beedell and Barbara Hargreaves

It's all a bit of a problem, but one that gives hours of fun.

Zap the bugs

INSECTICIDE

Rhubarb leaves are highly poisonous and can be made into an effective insecticide. Cut up 4 lb of rhubarb leaves and boil in 1 gallon of water for ½ hour. Strain off the leaves and let the liquid cool. Store in ridged bottled, clearly marked 'Poison' and well out of reach of children. Before use, dissolve 4 oz of soft soap in 4 pints of hot water. When the water has cooled, add about 1 pint of rhubarb solution. Spray to destroy greenfly and blackfly. This liquid is highly poisonous – do not spray on fruit or veg. Keep away from children. Ibid.

CATERPILLAR EXTERMINATOR

For this you need to save up or acquire ½ lb of filter cigarette ends. Boil them in 1 gallon of water for ½ hour. Drain. Keep liquid in stoppered bottle for a few weeks. Dilute with 4 parts of water to 1 of nicotine mixture. Spray on to roses. (Warning: This is poisonous – keep away from the fruit and vegetables.) When you see what the nicotine does to the caterpillars, you may stop smoking. Keep away from children.

From *1001 Ways of Saving Money*, Tony Swindells

MILLIPEDE AND WIREWORM TRAPS

Take a tall tin can and punch holes in it. Fill with vegetable and fruit peelings. Plant it upright in flower border with wire handle sticking out to mark the spot. Millipedes and wireworms are not very bright and will move in as squatters. Lift the can out of the ground once a week and burn contents.

Ibid.

Suddenly I'm getting a bit sorry for the pests. Time, then, to move on out of the cultivated areas and into the fields. How about a bracing walk?

Into the fields

Let's do it. And after the happy, jolly, healthy free walk let's pitch a tent in some bosky glade. Are you concentrating? Then breathe deeply, grasp a strut firmly in each hand, and begin.

The ridge pole is threaded through loops sewn onto the ridge of the tent, and when the ridge pole is positioned on the spikes of the upright poles, the tent is automatically slung below the ridge pole, the distance below being determined by the length of the loops on the tent ridge. This system is only practicable when the tent has no bell-end.
From *Modern Camping*, Alan Ryalls

Or, rather than wrestling with a ridge-tent, you could try a patrol tent.

The patrol tent does not have a sewn-in groundsheet. Instead there is a sod-cloth sewn into the bottoms of the walls...

I don't know why, but this sounds faintly sinister. Let's go back and see how the ridge tent is getting on.

Each leg, which is usually in three parts, has each part linked by a short spring to the part with which it marries. The springs, which are clipped into the open ends of each tube, are by no means unbreakable, but they can be replaced if necessary, with the aid of a simple spring inserter.
Ibid.

Happy days! If all else fails, just remember that:

It is easy to organize a small cheese and wine party to while away a rainy evening in camp.
Ibid

The mind boggles. On second thoughts, let's go and do something else. Like bird-watching. From a car.

Bird-watching (unconventional)

Now we meet a bird-watcher who has a light-bulb moment. After driving to a prime birding spot, alighting and spending cold hours shivering with binoculars underneath a dripping thorn bush, he suddenly realizes that help is at hand, in the shape of his warm, weatherproof conveyance.

It may come as a surprise that the car, slaughterer and wreaker of devastation, is as good a barrier as any. There's no more convenient or comfortable place from which to watch birds. I was heading homewards in a car when I saw my first red-backed shrike, perched contemptuously on the very top of one of the roadside hawthorns where I had searched for it on foot all afternoon.
From *The Roadside Wildlife Book*, Richard Mabey

Isn't that great? And there is more.

Hide – and bird-table too. In frost or deep snow you can park your car at the edge of a wood, sprinkle nuts and seed on the bonnet and sit and wait for the show to begin on the other side of the windscreen... Not only the usual tits and greenfinches have been known to come and feed on car bonnets in these conditions, but nuthatches, woodpeckers and even hawfinches.

Ibid.

So now we know what those steamed
up cars waiting quietly in really rural
parts are doing. They are waiting for
woodpeckers to come and feast on their
bonnets. Believe that, believe anything.

Our car-bound birdwatcher, being
British, feels a twinge of guilt.

*I still remember with some shame the
day I spent watching the spring wader
migration in north Norfolk from inside
a comfortable saloon, keeping the
visibility up with the windscreen wipers.
Insulating yourself out of sheer laziness
from the rigours of the outdoors is not the
way to get to grips with wild creatures.
Ibid.*

How appalling to be warm and dry while
pursuing your hobby. Better move rapidly
on to fishing, where insulating yourself from
the rigours of the outdoors while getting
to grips with wild creatures would be just
about impossible.

To the riverbank

In fishing not everything can be perfect. Wet blank days and soggy socks, icy east wind and tangled tackle can be recalled.

From *Memoirs of a Ghillie*, Gregor MacKenzie

That's more like it, especially the soggy socks. Suffer for your sport! But steady on, the river bank is getting lively.

Men who are distinguished, dignified by manners and fine clothing, august leaders in legal and commercial life are often transformed into a cross between a scampering schoolboy and a tenuous Tarzan just by that intoxicating tug. The judge, a thesaurus of measured, precise phrases in his head, becomes at one with an enraged docker screaming profanities at the top of his voice as a line snags.

Ibid.

Now that would be worth seeing.

SUCCESSFUL FISHING

Old Matthew, walking home from his fishing, was wearing the expression that only anglers know. The brow had mislaid some furrows, the eyes were not yet quite back with the world, the shoulders had slacked their tension. The wee laddie, myself, piped up to him: 'And did ye hae a guid day?'

Matthew grinned, a little dreaming still left round his mouth. He paused and then, 'Ay sonny I did that. I have fished successfully all day and caught nothing.'
It took much time and fishing before I fully understood his point.
Ibid.

Old Matthew probably had not been rained on for the afternoon. That would make anybody's shoulders slack their tension.

RIPARIAN RIGHTS

Do you ever find yourself wide awake at night, wondering what your riparian rights are? You need wonder no longer.

Riparian Rights are the rights recognized by law of a landowner in respect of a natural stream flowing either through or alongside his land. When 'alongside' applies he has the rights up to mid-stream. These natural rights include the exclusive right of fishing in the waters, and this enables him to licence others, whether members of an angling association or specified individuals, to fish in the waters. The right given by the licence carries with it a right of reasonable access to the waters.

From *The Complete Guide to Country Living*, Suzanne Beedell and Barbara Hargreaves

Feeling more relaxed now? Splendid.

AND ON TO THE SEASHORE

Sticking with fish, this time we have mullet being shared out in Cornwall.

On being brought ashore, the fish is thrown on to the ground in piles, each pile being as nearly equal as the men can conveniently make it. Generally there are two piles to each man. When all the fish has been divided thus, one of the men goes round with a basket, and into it the others throw some little personal belonging, such as a knife, a tobacco box or the like. These are then thrown out at random on to the piles of fish, by which means each man is able to identify his share and feels, moreover, that he has received a fair and impartial allotment.

From *Cornwall and its people*, A. K. Hamilton Jenkins

A good trick to remember next time you are (for example) dividing out a meal for a large family.

Weather

Whatever you are doing in the rural outdoors, weather will come into the equation. The difference between doing almost anything outside on a gloriously warm day as compared to a freezing, overcast day with a strong sou'wester hitting you right between the shoulder blades has to be experienced to be believed. Time to examine some clear-sighted weather forecasting garnered by David Bowen in *Britain's Weather*.

If the moon rises haloed round,
Soon you'll tread on deluged ground.

An abundance of grass snakes is a sign of
rain.

Hark! I hear the asses bray;
We shall have some rain today.

When you observe smoke from the
chimney of a house descend upon the
roof and pass along the eaves, expect rain
within six hours.

When the voices of blackbirds are
unusually shrill, rain will follow.

When woodpeckers are much heard, rain
will follow.

If the cock goes crowing to bed,
He'll certainly wake with a watery head.

Do you know what, I think it's going to rain! And somebody shut those birds up.

And here are a couple of predictions from the impenetrable school of weather forecasting.

ON CANDLEMAS DAY IF THE THORNS HANG ADROP, YOU CAN BE SURE OF A GOOD PEA CROP.

And here's another.

When a lagas shows in the sky
'Tis fining up for dry.
From *West Country Words and Ways*,
K.C.Phillipps

Right… we'll keep a good look out. At least these seem to be more optimistic in tone.

And we'll finish with my personal favourite. The next time you are down in your vegetable garden, feeling slightly bored and wondering whether or not the moment has come to put the onion sets in, just give this a try.

If you can sit on the ground with your trousers down and it feels alright, sow your seeds and they will be up in three days.
From *Country Cottage Companion*, Peggy Cole

REALLY RURAL
RECIPES AND
REMEDIES

REALLY RURAL
RECIPES AND
REMEDIES

Britain has a rich tradition of rural cooking – think venison steak, apple crumble and clotted cream. And we have many herbal recipes that work well. However, for a walk on the wild side, there are also plenty of rural recipes now side-lined because of the ingredients, quantities, or because nowadays most people would unhesitatingly head for the nearest fast food outlet rather than sample a lambs' tail pie. There are also certain rural remedies that would be shunned by your GP. Some of these are gathered here to be marvelled at rather than sampled. For determined thrill seekers you could try nattlin pie, which has much in common with a budget sausage roll. We'll plunge straight in to recipes. Read on, and enjoy.

Strange ingredients

ROOK PIE

Skin and draw the rooks, taking care not to break the gall-bladder. Divide into pieces, soak in milk for several hours. Put in dish with a little chopped beef, salt and pepper and a little butter. Cover with paste made with flour and water. Bake in slow oven for two hours. Cool, remove paste, and fill up with stock and cover with puff paste. Bake in hot oven till brown. Serve cold.

From *Tuppenny Rice and Treacle*, Doris E Coates

Feeling peckish? Or just slightly nauseous? Let's try lambs'tails.

LAMBS' TAIL PIE

Pluck the wool off the lambs'tails or scald them in boiling water in order to make the job easier. Place the tails in a large pot with some root vegetables and simmer until they are tender. Then put them in a pie dish with chopped hard-boiled eggs and parsley. Add a little stock and cover with a pastry lid. Cook in an oven until golden.

These are the tails that have been docked off young lambs. The modern method is not to cut them off but to bind the tails and let them rot off. From *Granny's Cookery Book*, Frances Kitchin

Somehow the informative note doesn't help at all.

The Cornish housewife

Cornish housewives had original ideas, and everything was grist that came to their mill. Nothing was too big or too small, too tough or too greasy. Nothing was considered too 'common or unclean' to compose a Cornish pie. Proof of this may be seen in the mackerel pies, pilchard pies, conger pies, bream pies, ram pies, muggety pies, taddago pies, nattlin pies, curlew pies, squab pies, lammy pies, giblet pies, leek pies, 'tatty' pies, 'herby' pies, and many more that formerly graced the tables of old Cornwall.

From *Cornwall and its People*, A K Hamilton Jenkins

Has this prepared you for what comes next? Gracing the table is that old Cornish favourite, starry-gazy pie.

STARRY-GAZY PIE

Of all the various fish pies, that made from pilchards was certainly the most odd. This pie went by the nick-name of 'starry-gazy', from the fact that the fish were cooked therein whole, with their heads projecting through the crust and their eyes goggling towards the ceiling! A stranger on one occasion eating starry-gazy pie is said to have exclaimed with some astonishment at the hardness of the fish's backbone. 'Let me see, my dear!' cried the woman, coming forward to the table, 'why that edn' no fish bone at all. That's our little Johnny's hair comb, what he lost two days ago – careless little emp!'

From *Cornwall and its People*, A K Hamilton Jenkins

SOME STRANGE OLD ENGLISH DISHES

Swan with Chawdron
Crane with Cretney
Heronusen with his Sique
Rabett Sowker
Larkes ingrayled
Pekoke in Hakell
Egrets in Boerwetye
Pigeons transmogrified
Mumbled rabbits

From *Recipes of Old England*, Bernard N Bessunger

I don't have a clue how to ingrayle a lark, in fact I don't even want to think about it. However I can share with you the method of mumbling rabbits: you cook them, tear them into very small pieces, and serve them on sippets. Sippet-making remains shrouded in mystery.

The book says encouragingly that these were flavoured with parsley, pepper and salt, and often enriched by the addition of cream. Then it adds, in a mystified tone, that the pies do not enjoy the same popularity as formerly. Entrails versus pizza. It's a close call.

MORE CORNISH PIES

Muggety pie: entrails of sheep or calves

Nattlin pies: entrails of pigs

YET MORE CORNISH PIES

Taddago pie: prematurely born sucking pigs

Lammy pie: stillborn or overlaid lambs

Lammy pie was apparently once the favourite 'feasten' dish of a parish in the neighbourhood of Penzance. A parish which I hope by now has welcomed in a gastro pub with open arms.

BEESTINGS CUSTARD

Take a pint of beesting and put in a pie dish. Add a pinch of salt and 4 tablespoons of sugar. Stir well and place in a moderate oven until set.

Beesting is the milk from a cow that has just calved.
From *Granny's Cookery Book*, Frances Kitchin

Too…much… information.

WEST COUNTRY METHOD OF CURING HAMS

Take 3 or 4 hams weighing 14 or 16 lbs each. Let them hang for a day, then rub well into each one 2 oz of sal prunella, 2 oz saltpetre and a lb of salt. Put the hams into a deep pan and rub then each day for 3 days. Make a pickle by boiling together 3 gallons of water, 4 lbs of common salt, 4 lbs of bay salt and 7 lbs of moist sugar. Skim thoroughly and when the pickle has boiled for 20 minutes, pour it hot over the meat. The hams must be rubbed and turned daily and their relative position altered, the one on top being put to the bottom and so on. At the end of 3 weeks they must be drained, dried and smoked.

Bay salt is large crystals made from two kinds of salt. One is prepared by evaporation from sea-water and the other by evaporation from salt springs and lakes. Saltpetre is used to redden the meat. Sal prunella is a preparation of fused nitre.

From *Granny's Cookery Book,* Frances Kitchin

Not the done thing

At this stage it would be easy to sympathise with the writer who simply couldn't bring himself to write out the 'frightful recipe 'To roast a shoulder of Mutton in Blood'!' Or with a lady called Mrs Pascoe, who expressed shrinking horror as she observed shellfish being served at the dinner table.

Chacun à son goût…but it strikes me as shockingly fee-fa-fumish to see a supper party picking these creatures out with a pin and gobbling them down, 'scholar's hats' and all.

From *Cornwall and its People*, A.K. Hamilton Jenkins

Well, yes. But, as she says, each to their own taste.

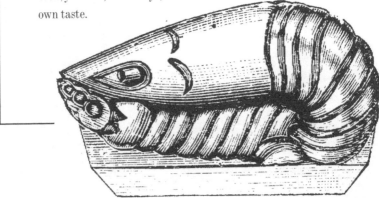

CRABSCOE OF CRAWFISH

Take about a Quarter of an Hundred or more of Crawfish, take out the tails then pound the shells very fine, then put them in a stewpan with about a Pound of good butter, set it over a gentle Fire and let it stew a good while, then strain the Butter into another Stewpan and let it stand to be cold, then work it to a Cream with a wooden Ladle or Spoon, then by Degrees add to it yolks of Eggs, the crumb of a french Roll steep'd in Cream, a little Lemon Peel and Nutmeg, if you have it sweet add a little Sugar and work it all together well with a little Cream, then make a Rim of Paste round the Dish put in your Ingredients, stick the tails of your Crawfish in it and so bake it – half an Hour bakes it.

From *Recipes of Old England,*
Bernard N Bessunger

Healthy appetites

Quite apart from the enormous mounds of ingredients, the sheer quantity of food consumed in former years can often surprise. Here is the description of a family crisis.

Mrs Newton, the mistress, rushes into the kitchen with the alarming news: 'My husband has brought two clients of his, and is anxious to show them some hospitality. They leave by the six o'clock train; it is now nearly three. What can be got for their dinner that may be quickly done?' With only three hours to prepare a hurried snack, Miss Severn (the lady-help) does not panic: 'Salmon and caper sauce, lamb and mint sauce, mutton cutlets, young carrots, and potatoes, will not be a bad impromptu dinner, for they can't expect anything else, except sweets... We can have stewed rhubarb and macaroni cheese.'

From *A Diet of Tripe*, Terence McLaughlin

If that was an impromptu snack, what on earth would they have sat down to on a normal day? A vast vat of Crabscoe of Crawfish perhaps.

Time to cater for the smaller appetite.

SPARROW PIE

Pluck and draw the birds and stuff them with some veal forcemeat. Line the bottom and sides of a pie-dish with thin slices of steak. Put in the birds, cut in halves. Season with salt and pepper and intersperse with sections or slices of hardboiled eggs. Half-fill the dish with stock, cover with shortcrust pastry and bake in a moderately hot oven for about 1½ hours, depending on the size.

From *Food from the Wild*, Judy Urquhart

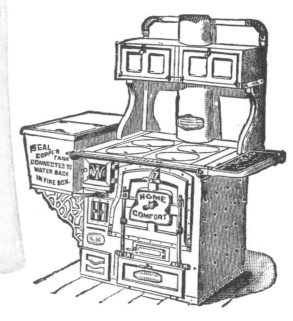

A sparrow is a sparrow. Chirp. But the next section of recipes is concerned with making things seem other than they are. Which was, let's face it, a sound idea.

Have you guessed what it is yet?

IMITATION GROUSE

Place half a red herring into the inside of a cleaned pigeon, roast in the usual way, basting well. Take out the herring before serving.

From *Granny's Cookery Book*, Frances Kitchin

POOR MAN'S GOOSE

1 lb liver, 1 large onion, 6 oz streaky bacon, 3 oz stuffing made from onion and sage, 2 oz lard or butter, little flour, seasoning, ½ pint of stock.

Cut the liver into 1/2-inch slices and dust with the flour. Melt the fat and fry the liver long enough just to seal it, remove and allow to cool. Place the stuffing on top of the liver and twist the bacon around each slice to secure the stuffing. Place in an ovenproof dish, pour a little of the fat on top and pour the stock around the sides. Cook in a moderate oven for 20 minutes and then remove the lid. Continue to cook for another 10 minutes.

From *Granny's Cookery Book*, Frances Kitchin

This recipe is sometimes called 'Mock Goose' and uses heart instead of liver. Then the heart is left whole and stuffed.

SALMON SUBSTITUTE

Bar or dog fish (don't be put off by the name!) can be used successfully in any recipes in place of salmon.

From *1001 Ways of Saving Money*, Tony Swindells

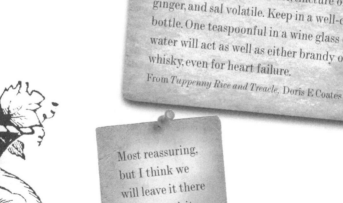

VEAL SWEETBREAD LIKE HEDGEHOGS

Scald the sweetbreads, and lard them with ham and truffles, cut in small lardoons, and fried for a short time in butter (lard them so that the lardoons may stick out a little to give the appearance of bristles); simmer the sweetbread thus larded in the same butter the lardoons were fried in, with stock, a glass of white wine, seasoned with a little salt, and pepper; when done, skim and strain the sauce, add a little *cullis,* and serve this over the sweetbreads.

From *Recipes of Old England*

After witnessing the arrival on the dinner table of sweetbreads dressed up as hedgehogs (or vice versa), you might need a good swig of the following restorative elixir, to bring you round again.

SUBSTITUTE FOR BRANDY, OR WHISKY

Equal parts of chloric ether, tincture of ginger, and sal volatile. Keep in a well-corked bottle. One teaspoonful in a wine glass of water will act as well as either brandy or whisky, even for heart failure.

From *Tuppenny Rice and Treacle,* Doris E Coates

Most reassuring, but I think we will leave it there and go to visit some plant life

The rural vegetarian

Until recently, the rural vegetarian had a hard time of it. They were expected to tuck in gratefully to their delicious slice of muggetty pie and if they pushed away their plate and reached for a vegetarian option, they were regarded with deep suspicion. In *A Diet of Tripe* Terence McLaughlin took a dubious view of vegetarians, with their 'abstinence from meat or insistence on sea-salt, wholefoods or yang foods…' and then found himself in possession of one of their magazines. It did not make happy reading for him.

In the contents list of one of the magazines dealing with wholefoods and non-processed diet, I found the following grouping, with nothing to suggest that they were not all normal aspects of diet: 'Parsley – all-year-round vegetable', composting, vegetarian recipes, how to manage a small non-mechanized farm, keeping a goat…and then, at the end, 'Fairies, the hidden world of nature spirits'.

Good grief! It was enough to send a chap snorting off to put in a double order for Roast Shoulder of Mutton in Blood. However, times change and though we must put the spirit world of fairies regretfully to one side, we can contribute some vegetarian recipes.

NETTLES

Picked when they first appear, nettle tops cooked in salted water with a knob of butter taste a little like spinach. If they are too old, they have the texture of (one imagines) gritty, furry caterpillars.

From *The Complete Guide to Country Living*, Suzanne Beedell and Barbara Hargreaves

Oh dear, that won't do. Try again.

NETTLES AGAIN

I have often heard that young nettles, cooked until tender in salted water, make a vitamin-rich substitute for spinach at a time in early spring when a change of vegetable is welcome. We tried this on the family and got a thumbs-down reception. The flavour was insipid and the texture fibrous and coarse.

From *Cowpasture*, Roy Lacey

No, that doesn't sound great either. Third time lucky.

EVEN MORE NETTLES

Nettles (would you believe?) are as tasty and nutritious as spinach – and they're free! All you need is a good pair of gloves. Pick the young, tender nettles. Wash well in salted water, still wearing the gloves. Cook in just a few tablespoons of water with a knob of butter, salt and pepper. The result is a delicious puree, very like spinach.

From *1001 Ways of Saving Money*, Tony Swindells

Success at last! And by the sound of it, nettles

Some more vegetarian ideas

Now, while we're riding high, is the time to explore some more vegetarian ideas.

OLIVES

Many of the people here had never seen an olive tree before, and were curious about its fruit: so I gave them olives to try. One comment was: "Well, Mrs —'d never have christened her daughter Olive, if her'd a-tasted one of they."

From *West Country Words and Ways* by K.C. Phillipps

MUSHROOMS

It is quite an elegant treat to braise a handful of fresh mushrooms in butter and use in place of carrots. Pure sylvan drama if you know what you're doing out in the woods at mushroom time.

From *Super Natural Cookery* by Jim Corlett

If, on the other hand, you didn't know what you were doing out in the woods at mushroom time, and fancied a glass of wine with your *Coprinus atramentarius* risotto, you could come badly unstuck.

Coprinus atramentarius. Like its better-known cousin (ink cap) it is perfectly edible — provided no alcohol is drunk with the meal which includes it. In this combination it has a strange effect on the taker: a short time afterwards he begins to feel sick and his face, and occasionally his neck and arms, turn purple.

From *The Roadside Wildlife Book* by Richard Mabey

Perfectly edible then, except for the queasily turning purple bit. I say again, don't try this at home! In fact I think we'll leave it there with vegetarian recipes. Time to turn our attention to the great British picnic.

The Great British picnic

COMPARE AND CONTRAST

THE WORKING MAN'S PICNIC
Bread and butter was made up in a
handkerchief, with a sprinkling of
tea and sugar. Sometimes there was a
little potato pie with a few pieces of fat
bacon on it.

From *Picnics,* Jackie Gurney

A PICNIC WHICH TOOK PLACE IN THE SUMMER OF 1878

The gentry made their way down to Swallowcombe Park…
overlooking the lake, where the picnic was laid out. The hot food was
sent down in hay boxes, and the cold food kept in the Ice House at
the top of the Wilderness until wanted… The menu included chilled
game soup, veal rolls, fresh salmon, chicken in aspic, ham in aspic,
cold baron of beef, salads, framboises a la crème, Adelaide trifle,
strawberries and cream and ice puddings.

From *Picnics*, Jackie Gurney

And how about something to
drink? Mrs Beeton had strong
ideas on the refreshment needed
for a picnic, and she was a lady
who never did things by halves.
This picnic is planned for 40
people, but even so the quantities
seem more than adequate.

Beverages – 3 dozen quart bottles of ale,
packed in hampers; ginger-beer, soda-water,
and lemonade, of each 2 dozen bottles; 6 bottles
of sherry, 6 bottles of claret, champagne à
discrétion, and any other light wine that may
be preferred, and 2 bottles of brandy.

From *Picnics*, Jackie Gurney

It is all reminiscent of Mole and Ratty's picnic in *The Wind in the Willows*.

'What's inside it?' asked the Mole, wriggling with curiosity.

'There's cold chicken inside it,' replied the Rat briefly; 'coldtonguecoldhamcoldbeef-pickledgherkinssaladfrenchrollscress-sandwichespottedmeatgingerbeerlemonade-sodawater-' 'O stop, stop,' cried the Mole in ecstasies: 'This is too much!'

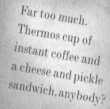

Far too much. Thermos cup of instant coffee and a cheese and pickle sandwich, anybody?

THE ECOLOGICALLY SOUND MUMMY

Mandy wants to help save the planet. She really, really does. All her cleaning products come out of ecologically sound bottles in reassuring shades of pastel green. She's put foil down the back of the radiators and bought new thick curtains (expensive but so gorgeous). Now she really ought to turn down the radiators too but she's taking it one step at a time. James isn't a convert yet and has completely drawn the line at her suggestion of fitting a composting loo into the downstairs bathroom. He says it's bad enough bashing your head on all the door lintels as you feel your way around the house in the half-hour of gloom before the energy-saving light bulbs get going, without lifting the loo lid to display a seething mass of bacteria. So Mandy salves her conscience by clothes-shopping in charity *(continues overleaf)*

shops (nice ones, in Newbury), and making her own pasta. She grows
sage for the children's colds, echinacea for their immune systems
and chamomile to calm James down when he hears her proposal to
build their drawing-room extension out of wattle and daub. Mandy
tried not washing her hair to save on the shampoo slicks spiralling
down into the aquifers but after two weeks she really couldn't
bear it any longer. There are limits. As she sorts all the rubbish into
different bags and sets off for the dump in her mighty 4x4 (because
she will not compromise on the children's safety) she is happily
planning a home business bottling baby's pure fruit purée on her
kitchen table.

For the last word on diet, let's turn
to the medical profession. Here is Dr
Parry, with a fine recommendation:

*The active professional man should
invariably exhilarate daily, and always,
if possible, with wine.*

Top plan!

Rural economies

It is time to stagger away from the mounds of plenty, and contemplate some thrift. We are told that one-third of food bought today will end up uneaten in a landfill site. Let us rewind the clock for some practical and possibly edible food recycling ideas.

Slice stale fruit cake thinly, dampen with sherry and bake between thin layers of pastry. Cut into squares.

From *1001 Country Household Hints*, Mary Rose Quigg

Keep cabbage and cauliflower stumps – grate and mix with grated onion and mayonnaise for an inexpensive coleslaw.

Ibid.

Crisp limp lettuce and celery by placing in a pan of cold water for an hour with slices of raw potato, or a piece of washed coal.

From *1001 Country Household Hints*, Mary Rose Quigg

If you throw away the peelings from an apple or potato, you throw away its most nutritious part. Instead, make sure the peelings are clean. Mince. Use.

From *1001 Ways of Saving Money*, Tony Swindells

Old, rejected sandwiches look very sad. Cheer them up by coating in batter. Fry and serve hot.

Ibid

A CAUTIONARY VERSE FROM THE SECOND WORLD WAR

Auntie threw her rinds away.
To the lock-up she was taken.
There she is and there she'll stay
Till she learns to save her bacon!

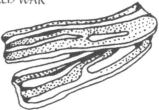

And if the meat is a bit whiffy? No problem at all, you can eat it anyway with the aid of a couple of hot hints from the past.

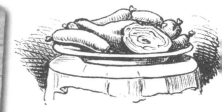

The best method for sweetening meat when tainted, either through forgetfulness or soft weather, is to put a few pieces of charcoal, each about the size of an egg, into the pot or saucepan with the meat or fish to be boiled.
From *Oh No Dear!*, Roy Hindle

If meat has really 'turned', the only thing you can do is burn it. But if it has only reached the stage of smelling very slightly high, it can be made perfectly edible simply by wiping it over with a clean cloth that has been dipped in vinegar.
From *1001 Ways of Saving Money*, Tony Swindells

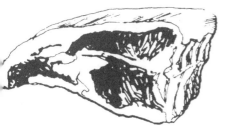

Boiled nettles, anyone?

Remedies, sovereign and otherwise

So now you've finished your helping of starry-gazy pie, with side order of dodgy mushrooms and a plate of beestings custard to follow. You've had your daily exhilaration. It's quite probably a suitable time to have a look at some really rural remedies. And if you decide to go and boil up some **Oil of Rats** in the potting shed, then feel a bit strange afterwards, and find yourself on the wrong end of a stomach pump in your local A&E department Don't Blame Me. We'll plunge straight into the deep end. Read on and enjoy.

The rural type tended towards toughness. Have a look at this tender warning from a book about salmon fishing on the Tweed.

Should you be of a delicate temperament and be wading in the month of February when it may chance to freeze very hard, pull down your stockings and examine your legs. Should they be black or even purple it might perhaps be as well to get on dry land; but if they are only rubicund, you may continue to enjoy the water.

From *Memoirs of a Ghillie*, Gregor MacKenzie

Those of a less delicate temperament can presumably watch their legs detach and go floating off down the river without turning a hair. Especially if they are on to a decent salmon.

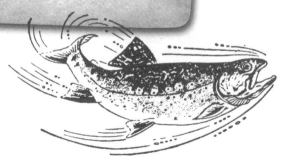

There's nothing common about a cold

For those soft enough to call in a bit of help in their fight to retain physical fitness, here are some suggestions.

SCENARIO 1: YOU HAVE A COLD

There is no certain cure for cold in the head. Camphor is recommended by some, while others have faith in the old-fashioned remedy of putting the feet in hot water and rubbing the nose with tallow, though it is not easy to get a candle of that material in every house now.

From *Oh No Dear!*, Roy Hindle

So there you are, sneezing mightily, smelling of moth balls, soaking your feet in hot water and rubbing your nose with a candle made of animal fat. Let us add to your miseries.

SCENARIO 2: YOU HAVE A COLD AND RHEUMATISM.

Some of the old women used to say that garters made from eel skins, if worn correctly, kept rheumatism away.

From *Memoirs of a Fen Tiger*, Audrey James

All right, we'll add some eel skin garters, worn correctly. But, alas, you have sat too long with your feet in hot water and to your horror you discover something else.

SCENARIO 3: YOU HAVE A COLD AND RHEUMATISM AND A BED SORE

The white of an egg beaten to a stiff froth; add two tablespoons of spirits of wine. Apply occasionally with a feather.

From *Tuppenny Rice and Treacle*, Doris E Coates

No, that's enough. We will examine the rest of the remedies from a safe distance.

REMEDY FOR BOILS

Place one teaspoonful of gunpowder in a good thick fig. Eat one three times a day before meals until the boils disappear. N B Safe and sure.

From *Tuppenny Rice and Treacle*, Doris E Coates

Really? I'm sure the boils would be blown away, but what about the rest of you?

REMEDIES FOR WARTS

(there were a great many. I offer you the strangest)

Do not laugh at this, but I have on several occasions cured warts on animals – and people – by the following procedure. Take an apple, cut it in half and rub one half over and into the warts. Tie the apple together again with string (rather 'fiddly') and hang on a tree or bush. Do not touch the warts again, or if possible, look at them – but in due time when the apple has withered the warts will be gone.

Steal a small piece of raw beef from the larder, rub it on all the warts and then bury it in the garden. As the meat rots, so the warts rot.

Touch the wart with an ordinary garden slug…

A doctor, who shall be nameless, when asked to cure a wart asked despairingly, 'Have you tried hitting them with a Bible?'

From *A Guide to Country Living*, P.D.N. Earle

REMEDIES FOR CRAMP
(this was another popular complaint)

Stand barefoot on a cork bath mat, but this has the disadvantage that you have to get out of bed and may catch cold in the process.

A circlet of corks to go around the leg or a cork tied on with a silk handkerchief or kept on with a silk stocking also helps.

On retiring to bed turn slippers upside down. This may sound farcical but is known to have cured sufferers and costs nothing.

A friend who suffered from cramp always filled her bed with corks. When she was taken ill the doctor called and found the corks. She was very crestfallen when he lectured her on the evils of drink!

From *A Guide to Country Living*, P.D.N. Earle

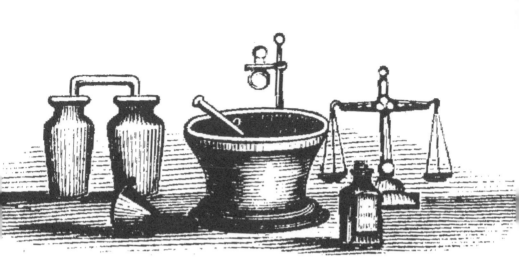

REMEDY FOR POISONED WOUNDS

(only one offered this time, but it does rather linger in the mind)

A pounded-up mixture of 'bullorns' (snails) and groundsel was used as a poultice for
gatherings or poisoned wounds.

From *Cornwall and its People*, A.K. Hamilton Jenkins

Regrettably the joint recipe
for curing whooping cough and
also destroying caterpillars on
gooseberry bushes has been
lost to posterity.

A CORNISH CURE-ALL

And it sounds highly likely that the recipe for 'Dutch oil' also went to the grave with its maker.

There was a certain mixture known in the Camborne district as 'Dutch oil', a few drops of which, taken on sugar, was regarded as a panacea for almost every kind of ill. This medicine was retailed by an old man who jealously guarded the secret of its preparation. At length one of his neighbours, who was an early riser, chanced to see him one morning in the garden diligently gathering worms. Seeing that in Cornwall the earthworm is commonly known as an 'angle-dutch' the making of this famous oil ceased from then to be regarded as a secret process!
From *Cornwall and its People*, A.K. Hamilton Jenkins

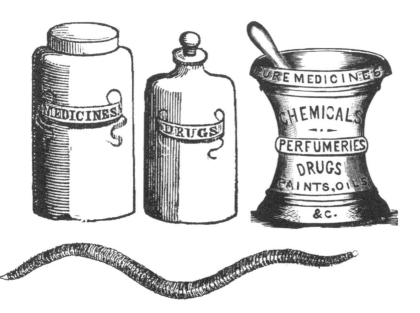

You never know when you might need this next and final remedy, and it follows on so nicely from the previous one.

RECIPE FOR THE ALLURING OF RATS

Twenty drops of aniseed, 10 drops of rhondium, 40 drops of oil of ambergris, 50 drops of musk, one root of valerian bruised, 20 drops of oil of rats.

'Oil of Rats'! This must be the ultimate really rural recipe.

ACKNOWLEDGMENTS

To the heroic band of country authors who have laboured unstintingly to record and explain the peculiarities of rural life. I salute you!'

Thanks also to Nicky Snell

INDEX

BIBLIOGRAPHY

Anne Andrews her Book, 1756

Archer, Fred, *The Cottage Life Book*, Newton Abbot: David & Charles, 1976

Archer, Fred, *The Countryman Cottage Life Book*, Newton Abbot: David & Charles, 1974

Baker, Margaret, *Folklore and Customs of Rural England*, Newton Abbot: David & Charles, 1974

Baker, Margaret, *Wedding Customs and Folklore*, Newton Abbot: David & Charles, 1977

Beedell, Susan & Hargreaves, Barbara, *The Complete Guide to Country Living*, Newton Abbot: David & Charles, 1979

Bell, Adrian, *Suffolk Harvest*, Newton Abbot: David & Charles, 1956

Bessunger, Bernard N., *Recipes of Old England*, Newton Abbot: David & Charles, 1973

Borst, Sally, *Self-Deficiency*, Newton Abbot: David & Charles, 1989

Bowen, David, *Britain's Weather*, Newton Abbot: David & Charles

Burton, Anthony, *The Shell Book of Curious Britain*, Newton Abbot: David & Charles, 1982

Campbell, B. & M., *The Countryman Animal Book*, Newton Abbot: David & Charles, 1973

Campbell, Margaret, Ed. *The Countryman Book of Humour*, Newton Abbot: David & Charles, 1975

Chapman, Chris, *The Right Side of the Hedge*, Newton Abbot: David & Charles, 1977

Christian, Roy, *Old English Customs*, Newton Abbot: David & Charles, 1972

Clark, Tim, *Margery Fish's Country Gardening*, Newton Abbot: David & Charles, 1989

Coates, Doris E., *Tuppenny Rice and Treacle*, Newton Abbot: David & Charles, 1975

Cole, Peggy, *Country Cottage Companion*, Newton Abbot: David & Charles, 1988

Cooper, Rosaleen, *Games from an Edwardian Childhood*, Newton Abbot: David & Charles, 1982

Corlett, Jim, *Super Natural Cookery*, Newton Abbot: David & Charles, 1974

Earle, P.D.N. Ed. *A Guide to Country Living*, Newton Abbot: David & Charles, 1971

Fish, Margery, *Cottage Garden Flowers*, Newton Abbot: David & Charles, 1980

Foyster, John & Proud, Keith, *Gamekeeper*, Newton Abbot: David & Charles, 1986

Gill, Crispin, Ed. *The Countryman's Britain*, Newton Abbot: David & Charles, 1976

Grahame, Kenneth, *The Wind in the Willows*, London: Penguin Popular Classics, 2007

Gurney, Jackie, *Picnics*, Newton Abbot: David & Charles, 1982

Hamilton Jenkins, A.K., *Cornwall and its People*, Newton Abbot: David &

Charles, 1945

arris, Mary Corbett, *Crafts, Customs and Legends of Wales*, Newton Abbot: David & Charles, 1980

art, Edward, *The Hill Shepherd*, Newton Abbot: David & Charles, 1977

arvey, Nigel, *A History of Farm Buildings in England and Wales*, Newton Abbot: David & Charles, 1970

ibbs, John, *The Country Chapel*, Newton Abbot: David & Charles, 1988

indle, Roy, *Oh No Dear!*, Newton Abbot: David & Charles, 1982

ames, Audrey, *Memoirs of a Fen Tiger*, Newton Abbot: David & Charles, 1986

itchin, Frances, *Granny's Cookery Book*, Newton Abbot: David & Charles, 1978

acey, Roy, *Cowpasture*, Newton Abbot: David & Charles, 1980

ewis, Lesley, *The Private Life of a Country House*, Newton Abbot: David & Charles, 1980

Lothian, Elizabeth, *Country House Cookery from the West*, Newton Abbot: David & Charles, 1978

Mabey, Richard, *The Roadside Wildlife Book*, Newton Abbot: David & Charles, 1974

MacKenzie, Gregor, *Memoirs of a Ghillie*, Newton Abbot: David & Charles, 1978

Manners, J.E., *Country Crafts Today*, Newton Abbot: David & Charles, 1974

McLaughlin, Terence, *A Diet of Tripe*, Newton Abbot: David & Charles, 1978

Peel J.H.B., *An Englishman's Home*, Newton Abbot: David & Charles, 1972

Phillipps, K.C., *West Country Words and Ways*, Newton Abbot: David & Charles, 1976

Quigg, Mary Rose, *1001 Country Household Hints*, Newton Abbot: David & Charles, 1994

Rundell, Mrs. *A New System of Domestic Cookery*, 1835

Ryalls, Alan, *Modern Camping*, Newton Abbot:

David & Charles, 1975

Spreckley, Val, *Keeping a Cow*, Newton Abbot: David & Charles, 1979

Swindells, Tony, *1001 Ways of Saving Money*, Newton Abbot: David & Charles, 1976

The Hiker and Camper magazine

Tourist in Wales, 1814

Urquhart, Judy, *Food from the Wild*, Newton Abbot: David & Charles, 1978

Ward, Sadie, *War in the Countryside*, Newton Abbot: David & Charles, 1988

Woodforde, John, *Furnishing a Country Cottage*, Newton Abbot: David & Charles, 1972

Wright, Philip A., *Old Farm Implements*, Newton Abbot: David & Charles, 1961